# Super Fun

## FAMILY
## CARD
## GAMES

# Super Fun FAMILY CARD GAMES

## 75 GAMES FOR ALL AGES

Corinne Schmitt

ROCKRIDGE
PRESS

For general information on our other products and services or to obtain technical support, please contact our Customer Care Department within the U.S. at (866) 744-2665, or outside the U.S. at (510) 253-0500.

Rockridge Press publishes its books in a variety of electronic and print formats. Some content that appears in print may not be available in electronic books, and vice versa.

Interior and Cover Design: Antonio Valverde

Photo Art Director/Art Manager: Samantha Ulban

Editor: Adrian Potts

Production Editor: Ashley Polikoff

Illustration © Samir Taiar, cover and back cover. All other images used under license © Shutterstock and © iStock.

ISBN: Print 978-1-64611-182-4 | eBook 978-1-64611-183-1

R0

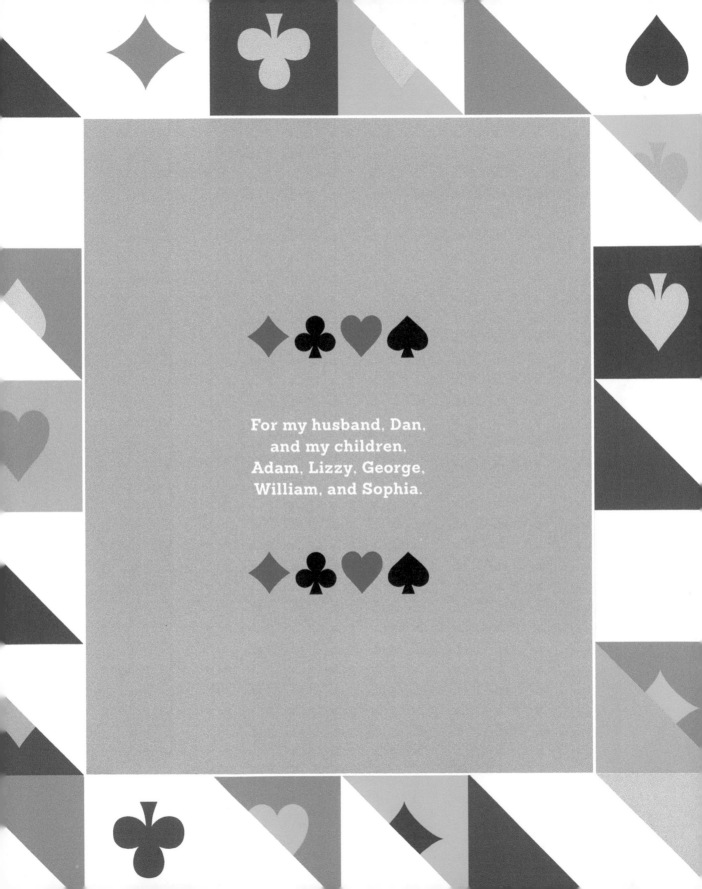

For my husband, Dan,
and my children,
Adam, Lizzy, George,
William, and Sophia.

# Contents

# Introduction

**W**hen it comes to easy, inexpensive entertainment, you can't beat a deck of cards. There are so many different card games, you could play a new one every day and never get bored. This collection of 75 card games is your guide to hours of family fun. I've included in this collection games for all ages, skill levels, and group sizes, so whether you have an only child or a big gang, you'll find plenty of games to enjoy.

I'm a firm believer in quality family time. My husband served 30 years in the Marine Corps, and that meant many relocations and separations. Early on, I realized our family's stability wasn't going to be a house or community, since those changed every few years. Instead, our family had to be its own anchor. So from the time my kids were very young, I've been committed to fostering a tribe within my family. We work together, play together, laugh together, and endure hardships together.

To create that family stability, I chose to be a stay-at-home mom. For me, this was the easiest way to provide consistency. The upside was plenty of time with my children. The downside was that we were a single-income family. As a result, when it came to family entertainment, I was always thinking frugally. And that's how I fell in love with card games.

Not only are playing cards inexpensive, they're easy to bring with you anywhere. And unlike portable electronics, card games facilitate conversation among players. It's so much more fun and rewarding to laugh and taunt each other over a game of Gin Rummy than to sit side by side staring at phones.

An added advantage of playing card games with your kids is that you get to sneak in lessons without them realizing they're learning. Several of the games in this book involve math, strategy, and problem-solving. Where applicable, I've highlighted the specific skills within the game details.

I've included several classic games from my childhood as well as new games my kids have taught me and some we've made up together. I hope you enjoy introducing your children (or grandchildren) to these games. Use the nostalgic games to share details about your childhood (kids love this!), and consider handing the book to them to let them teach you how to play a new game (they *really* enjoy being in charge).

No matter how you use this book or which games you choose to play, I hope you find several new ways to connect as a family and create fun memories together.

# WHAT YOU'LL NEED

All of the games in this book use a French or Anglo-American deck of cards, which is commonly known as a standard deck of cards. A standard deck has 52 cards—13 cards in four suits (spades, hearts, diamonds, and clubs). Each suit contains 13 cards: ace, 2, 3, 4, 5, 6, 7, 8, 9, 10, jack, queen, king. Many commercial decks also include jokers. Some games in this book will use the jokers, whereas others will specifically state that jokers should be removed. A few of the games make use of more than one deck of cards. The total number of decks needed is always clearly stated for each game.

In addition to cards, some games require other materials that you likely already have at home or that are easy to get. Typically, these items are for keeping score. When needed, those materials are listed at the beginning of the game.

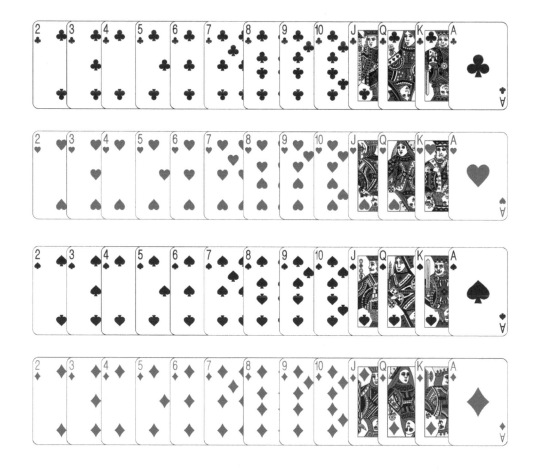

# CARD GAME BASICS

Card games have their own language and use particular terms and phrases to describe the cards themselves, the layout, and the manner of play. It's important for everyone to know what the terms mean so that everybody refers to things in the same way. Speaking the same language will help you avoid confusion and have more fun!

## Glossary

What follows is a glossary of all the terms you may come across in the games in this book. Refer back to these pages if you stumble across anything unfamiliar while playing.

### THE DECK

In each deck there are 13 cards in four suits, for a total of 52 cards.

- **FACE CARDS:** The jacks, queens, and kings (cards with characters that have faces)

- **RANK:** The value of each card relative to other cards in the same suit, typically in this order: 2, 3, 4, 5, 6, 7, 8, 9, 10, jack, queen, king, ace (though the ace is sometimes valued below the 2)

- **SUITS:** A grouping distinction, typically hearts, clubs, diamonds, and spades

### COMMON COMBINATIONS

Many card games require players to collect specific combinations of cards. These are the most common ones.

- **FLUSH:** A Poker hand consisting of any five cards in the same suit that are not in consecutive order (such as 2, 5, 6, 9, and queen of hearts)

- **FOUR OF A KIND:** Four cards of matching rank in different suits (such as 8 of clubs, 8 of spades, 8 of diamonds, and 8 of hearts)

- **FULL HOUSE:** A Poker hand consisting of one pair plus three of a kind (such as 7 of spades and 7 of diamonds, plus jack of clubs, jack of spades, and jack of diamonds)

- **PAIR:** Two cards of the same rank in different suits (such as 5 of hearts and 5 of clubs)

- **ROYAL FLUSH:** A Poker hand consisting of the 10, jack, queen, king, and ace, all in the same suit

- **RUNS:** Cards that are in a sequence of ascending rank (such as 3, 4, 5); a run can consist of three or more cards

- **STRAIGHT:** A Poker hand consisting of five cards in a run but not all in the same suit (such as 4 of clubs, 5 of hearts, 6 of diamonds, 7 of clubs, and 8 of spades)

- **SETS:** Cards that are all the same rank (such as 10s or 2s or kings)

- **STRAIGHT FLUSH:** A Poker hand consisting of five cards in a run, all in the same suit (such as 4, 5, 6, 7, and 8 of spades)

- **THREE OF A KIND:** Three cards of matching rank in different suits (such as 3 of clubs, 3 of spades, and 3 of diamonds)

- **TWO PAIRS:** A Poker hand consisting of two different pairs (such as 5 of hearts and 5 of clubs, plus ace of diamonds and ace of clubs)

## GENERAL CARD PLAY TERMS

- **BID:** A declaration of how many tricks or points a player expects to win during a round

- **CUT:** Lift a random number of cards from the top of the deck so that the dealer can place the cards beneath them on top

- **DEAL:** Pass out cards to each player after shuffling the deck; cards are dealt face down, unless otherwise specified in a particular game

- **DISCARD:** Dispose of a card or cards

- **DRAW:** Collect one or more cards

- **FOUNDATION:** The space where a player plays cards, typically building from a specific starting card through the remaining 12 ranks, either of the same suit or alternating between red and black cards, with the goal of playing all cards to piles in this area

- **HAND:** The cards a player holds that are not revealed to the other players

- **ROUND:** A phase of play in which every player has had a chance to play

- **SHUFFLE:** Mix at random the order of the cards in a deck

- **STOCK:** The cards from which a player can draw new cards during play

- **STOCKPILE:** The extra cards kept in reserve after the deal

- **TRICK:** A set of cards consisting of one card from each player in a round of play

- **TRUMP:** A suit of cards designated in a game to outrank all the other cards in the deck

- **TABLEAU:** The arrangement or layout of the cards on the table

- **WILD CARD:** A card that can represent any card of any suit and rank

# KEEP IN MIND

Card game rules are typically passed down from person to person and therefore evolve over time. As a result, there aren't really "official" rules for most card games. I've taken some liberties with the traditional rules of some games, made up standard deck versions of other games that are typically played with custom decks, and opted for some uncommon variations of a few games—all with the goal of providing you with a wide array of card games that are family-friendly. Because of this, it's important to read the instructions for each game carefully, as the version in this book may be different from the one you're familiar with.

One of the best things about playing games together as a family is making up your own rules and variations! I encourage you to experiment with different versions after you learn the basics.

# HOW TO USE THIS BOOK

To make it easier for you to find the kind of games you're looking for, this book is organized into three parts by number of players. Part 1 has games for two or more players. Part 2 has games for exactly two players. And Part 3 has single-player games—what's known as Solitaire. Within each part, the games are arranged in order of difficulty from easy to medium to hard.

I've labeled each game so you can quickly and easily identify if it's one you'll want to play. For each game you'll find:

- **DIFFICULTY:** Easy, medium, or hard

- **NUMBER OF PLAYERS**

- **FUN FOR WHAT AGES**

- **LENGTH OF PLAY FOR A TYPICAL GAME**

- **OBJECTIVE**

- **SKILL:** Because I believe we should make the most of any opportunity to foster learning, you'll find a label on some games that help develop a specific skill.

- **MATERIALS:** Whether certain cards should be removed from the deck and what else you might need to play the game

- **HOW TO DEAL:** How many cards each player gets and whether you deal them one at a time or in little groups

- **HOW TO PLAY:** How the game proceeds, including all the details you need to play the game

I really want this book to be a resource for fun game nights for your family, so throughout the book you'll find Family Game Night Tips. These are just simple ideas to help make your family playtime a little more special. For some games I've included a variation to help you kick-start your own version. And I've sprinkled some fun facts throughout the book. Look for the label Did You Know? to find them.

Ready to dive in and start playing? If you have younger kids, I recommend starting with Happy Families (page 8). Not only does the name of the game make me smile, but it's super simple to learn and play. For a quick and feisty game, try James Bond (page 9). You can play with up to six players, and each game takes only five minutes. When you're up for a longer game, try Too Many Monkeys (page 66), which is a great opportunity for everyone to act a little silly. Looking for a challenging game for older kids? Try Rook (page 89) and put everyone's strategy skills to the test.

# Part One

# GAMES FOR TWO OR MORE PLAYERS

# BLITZ

**TWO OR MORE PLAYERS**     **FUN FOR AGES:** 7+     |     **LENGTH OF PLAY:** 30 minutes

Also known as 31, Blitz is a fun combination of Blackjack, Texas Hold 'Em, and UNO. Kids will have fun catching erroneous knockers and won't even realize they're learning math while playing.

**OBJECTIVE:** Be the last player with a token     |     **SKILL:** Addition

**MATERIALS:**

◊ One deck of cards with jokers removed, three tokens per player (such as pennies, buttons, or candy)

## How to Deal

The dealer deals three cards to each player, one at a time. The remaining cards are placed in the middle of the table and will become the stock. One card is turned over and set beside the stock to begin the discard pile.

## How to Play

1. The player to the dealer's left draws a card from either the top of the stockpile or the top of the discard pile and adds it to their hand. In an effort to work toward a sum of 31 with cards that are all the same suit, the player then selects a card to discard. They place it face up on the discard pile. Play continues clockwise, with each player drawing one card from the top of either the stock or the discard pile and discarding one card.

2. When adding up the value of cards, only cards of the same suit are counted toward a player's score. The highest possible score for a three-card hand is 31, since aces are worth 11 points, face cards and 10s are each worth ten points, and every other card is worth its face value. If a player has three cards in different suits, only the highest-value card will stand as that player's score. If they have two cards in the same suit, they will add those values together to tally their score.

3. When a player believes they have the highest-value hand at the table, they knock on the table. All players then reveal their hands. If the player who knocked does indeed have the highest hand, they receive a token from the player with the lowest hand. If someone else has a higher hand than the player who knocked, the knocker must surrender a token to the center of the table. This token is now out of play. When a player runs out of tokens, they are out of the game. The last player with a token wins.

# CHEAT

**TWO OR MORE PLAYERS**     **FUN FOR AGES: 7+**   |   **LENGTH OF PLAY:** 10 minutes

Also known as I Doubt It, Cheat is a game that tests players' ability to bluff and detect deception.

**OBJECTIVE:** Get rid of all your cards

**MATERIALS:**

◊ One deck of cards with jokers removed

## How to Deal

The dealer deals out the cards, one at a time, to each player until either all cards have been distributed or no more cards can be dealt without leaving some players with more cards than others. Any extra cards are placed face down in the center of the table as the start of the discard pile.

## How to Play

1. The player to the left of the dealer begins by playing all the aces in their hand face down on the discard pile and declaring what has been played (for example, "two aces"). If the player has no aces, they can either pass or attempt to "cheat" by laying down one to four other cards but declaring them to be aces. The next player must then play all their 2s, the following player all their 3s, and so on. Players must be honest about the number of cards played (everyone can see them!) but can try to cheat by playing cards that aren't the correct value for the round. For example, a player starting with the hand in the picture (see page 5) will not be able to play a 4 if that number lands on their turn, so they may play a 6 instead but state "one 4," hoping they don't get caught, or "one 6," hoping nobody notices that ranks have been skipped.

2. Once the round reaches kings, play continues, beginning at aces again. If any player doubts another player's declaration, they proclaim "Cheat!" and the player who played the cards must reveal them. If the cards match what the player said they were, the challenger must pick up the entire discard pile. However, if the player was indeed cheating, they must pick up the discard pile instead.

# GO FISH

**TWO OR MORE PLAYERS**   **FUN FOR AGES: 4+**   |   **LENGTH OF PLAY:** 10 minutes

This classic matching game is easy enough for young children to play and fun for the whole family!

**OBJECTIVE:** Win the most books (four of a kind)   |   **SKILL:** Matching

**MATERIALS:**

◊ One deck of cards with jokers removed

## How to Deal

The dealer deals seven cards to each player for two or three players, or five cards for four or more players, one at a time. The remaining cards are spread out face down in the center of the table to form the fish pond or stock.

## How to Play

1. The player to the left of the dealer begins by asking any other player for a specific rank that matches any of the cards in their hand (for example, "Do you have any 2s?"). The player who was asked must give all their cards matching the request to the person who asked for them. The player who made the request can now ask another player (or the same player) for another rank that matches one in their hand. As long as the player's requests continue to be met with cards from the players they are asking, the player's turn continues. If the player being asked does not have any of the cards asked for, they say, "Go fish," and the player who made the request must draw a card from the fish pond, ending their turn. The next player to the left then begins their turn.

2. Whenever any player collects all four of a rank, they have made a book and can lay it face up in a pile in front of themselves. Play continues until all 13 books have been formed. The player with the most books wins.

# HAPPY FAMILIES

**TWO OR MORE PLAYERS**    **FUN FOR AGES: 4+**    |    **LENGTH OF PLAY:** 10 minutes

Happy Families, also known as Authors, is a British card game that is usually played with a custom deck depicting fun characters. It's very similar to Go Fish and is a great game for younger children.

**OBJECTIVE:** Collect the most happy families (sets of four of a kind)
**SKILL:** Matching

**MATERIALS:**

◊  One deck of cards with jokers removed

## How to Deal

The dealer deals out all the cards, one at a time.

## How to Play

1. The player to the dealer's left begins by asking another player for a card of a specific rank and suit (for example, "Do you have the 5 of diamonds?"). If the person who was asked has the card, they must give it to the asker. If the person who was asked does not have the card, the asker's turn ends and it is the next player's turn (play proceeds clockwise). On any turn, if an asker is successful in obtaining the desired card, they continue playing. Their turn ends only when the card they requested is not provided.

2. Whenever a player collects four cards of the same rank, they have formed a happy family and must set them face down in front of themselves. Play continues until all happy families have been formed. The player who has formed the most happy families wins.

# JAMES BOND

**TWO OR MORE PLAYERS**　　**FUN FOR AGES: 7+**　|　**LENGTH OF PLAY:** 5 minutes

This is a newer game that's really popular with kids. It's a quick-paced game that's easy to learn, so it's fun for the whole family.

**OBJECTIVE:** Get four of a kind in all of your piles

**MATERIALS:**

◊ One deck of cards with jokers removed (two decks for four to six players)

## How to Deal

The dealer deals four piles of four face-down cards to each player for three or six players, or six piles of four face-down cards for two, four, or five players (as shown in the picture on page 10). The remaining cards are placed face up in a row between the players.

## How to Play

1. To begin the game, the dealer yells, "Go!" Players pick up each of their piles, look at the four cards in the pile, and decide if they want to trade a card from the pile for one of the face-up cards in the center in an effort to create a pile of four of a kind. Players can only look at one of their piles at a time and can only replace one card at a time. They cannot trade cards directly from one pile to another. There are no turns. Everyone plays simultaneously. The first player to create matching sets of four in all of their piles yells, "James Bond!" to end the game.

**CONTINUED**

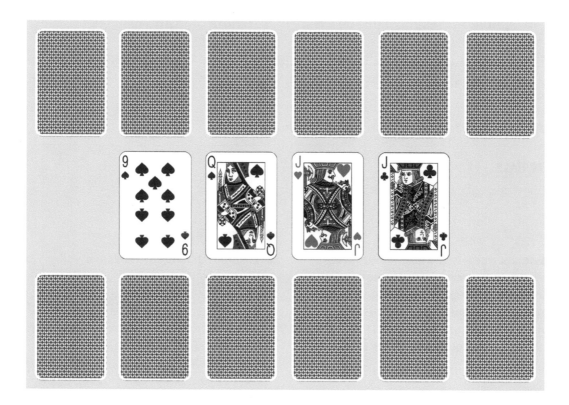

# MAKE 10

**TWO OR MORE PLAYERS**     **FUN FOR AGES: 7+**  |  **LENGTH OF PLAY:** 10 minutes

This game isn't about winning or losing—it's just a fun way to practice basic addition!

**OBJECTIVE:** Make as many combinations totaling ten as possible
**SKILL:** Addition

**MATERIALS:**

◊ One deck of cards with face cards, 10s, and jokers removed

## How to Deal

The dealer places 12 cards face up in the middle of the table, arranged in three rows of four cards each. The remaining cards are placed in a single pile face down next to the rows to form the stock.

## How to Play

1. The player to the dealer's left selects two cards from the exposed cards that equal ten when added together. The player removes the cards from the playing field and adds them to their pile. Two new cards are drawn from the stock to replace the missing cards in the playing field, and play continues clockwise until no more combinations of ten can be made.

**VARIATION:** For older kids, play the game as described, but have players also calculate the product of multiplying the two card values together.

# MEMORY

**TWO OR MORE PLAYERS**    **FUN FOR AGES: 4+**  |  **LENGTH OF PLAY:** 10 minutes

This classic game, also known as Concentration, is a great way to help kids learn to focus and improve their concentration skills.

**OBJECTIVE:** Collect the most matches  |  **SKILL:** Focus, memorization

**MATERIALS:**

◊ One deck of cards with jokers removed

## How to Deal

Lay out all the cards face down on the table in even rows.

## How to Play

1. The youngest player goes first. Players take turns flipping over two cards in an attempt to find matches in rank. When the rank of two cards matches, the player who turned them over removes them from the playing field and adds them to their pile.

2. Whenever a player reveals a match, they get to go again. Their turn does not end until the two cards revealed do not match. If the cards don't match, the player who revealed them turns them back over and play passes to their left. Play continues until all the cards have been removed from the playing field. The player with the most matches in their pile wins.

**VARIATION:** To increase the difficulty of the game, the cards have to match not only in rank but also in color.

# PIG

**FOUR OR MORE PLAYERS**     **FUN FOR AGES: 4+**   |   **LENGTH OF PLAY:** 20 minutes

Pig is such a fun and simple game that even very young children can play it. Because it works with large groups, it's a great party game, too.

**OBJECTIVE:** Be the last player still in the game

**MATERIALS:**

◊ One deck of cards with jokers removed

## How to Deal

The cards are sorted into 13 piles of four of a kind. The dealer collects as many piles as there are players (for example, in a five-player game, the dealer picks up five piles). The remaining piles are set aside and will not be used. The dealer shuffles together the piles they collected and deals four cards to each player, one at a time.

## How to Play

1. All players look at their cards and select a card they want to discard. Simultaneously, each player sets their discard next to the player to their left, then picks up the card passed to them from the right. Again, players look at their hands to choose a new discard. Each player is trying to collect four cards of the same rank (for example, four kings). When a player collects four of a kind, that player touches their nose. Everyone else must then also touch their noses. The last player to place a finger on their nose is the "pig" and is out of the game.

CONTINUED

2. The cards are gathered up, one set of four of a kind is removed and set aside, and the deal passes to the left. Play continues until the final round when only two people remain and one player collects four of a kind, making them the winner and forcing the last opponent out of the game.

**VARIATION:** Instead of forcing players out when they are the last to touch their nose, each player collects one letter of the word PIG (written on index cards or pieces of scrap paper). A player isn't removed from the game until they have collected all three letters.

# ROLLING STONE

**FOUR TO SIX PLAYERS**     **FUN FOR AGES: 7+**   |   **LENGTH OF PLAY:** 15 minutes

This is a fun game that keeps you on your toes, because just when you think you are about to win, you can end up back at square one.

**OBJECTIVE:** Get rid of all your cards

**MATERIALS:**

◊ One deck of cards with jokers and all 2s through 6s removed for a four-player game, all 2s through 5s removed for a five-player game, or all 2s removed for a six-player game

## How to Deal

The dealer deals out all the cards, one at a time.

## How to Play

1. The player to the left of the dealer begins by playing a card face up in the middle of the table. Continuing clockwise, the next player must play a card of the same suit. If, at any time, a player cannot follow suit, they must pick up all the cards in the center and add them to their hand. They then play any card, other than the suit that was most recently played, to continue the round.

2. Play continues until one player has played all their cards. They win the game.

# SALUTE THE KING

**TWO OR MORE PLAYERS**    **FUN FOR AGES: 7+**   |   **LENGTH OF PLAY:** 15 minutes

This simple and silly game will have everyone laughing.

**OBJECTIVE:** Be the first player to get rid of all your cards
**SKILLS:** Attention, focus

**MATERIALS:**

◊ One deck of cards with jokers removed

## How to Deal

The dealer deals out all the cards, one at a time, until the entire deck has been distributed. It doesn't matter if some players have more cards than others. Each player then stacks their cards into a single pile that remains face down in front of them.

## How to Play

1. Starting with the player to the left of the dealer and proceeding clockwise, each player turns over one card from their pile and immediately places it in the center of the table. If at any time specific cards are revealed, every player must immediately perform a required action. For example:

   • When an ace is played, all players must stand up.

   • When a king is played, all players must salute.

   • When a queen is played, all players must place their left hands over their hearts and bow their heads.

   • When a jack is played, all players must applaud.

2. The last person to perform the required action must pick up all the cards from the middle. Play then continues until somebody plays all their cards, becoming the winner.

# FAMILY GAME NIGHT TIP

**CHOOSING THE FIRST PLAYER**

Sometimes the hardest part of getting family game night started is getting past the decision of who will deal or play first. Sometimes it's because everyone is trying to be agreeable and so doesn't want to claim what they believe is a valued role. Other times it's because everyone wants the coveted role! No matter what the cause of the indecision, here are some simple, drama-free ways to choose:

- Play rock-paper-scissors.

- Draw random cards; high card wins.

- Write each player's name on a scrap piece of paper, put them all in a bag, and draw a name.

- On the count of three, everyone holds up 0 to 5 fingers. Then you can either:

  ◊ Add up the total and divide by the number of players. Whoever held up that number goes first, or

  ◊ Eliminate any players holding up the same number. The remaining player with the highest number goes first.

In games with multiple rounds or turns, the dealer or first player can change based on any of the following orders:

- From youngest to oldest

- By birth month from January to December (and day if two players are born in the same month)

- From A to Z using the first letter of each person's first name

- From shortest to tallest

- In rainbow order (red, orange, yellow, green, blue, indigo, violet) using shirt color

# SLAPJACK

**TWO OR MORE PLAYERS**    **FUN FOR AGES: 4+**   |   **LENGTH OF PLAY:** 20 minutes

Slapjack is a fast-paced, family-friendly game that gets very playful and loud as players race each other to slap the jacks and win the cards.

**OBJECTIVE:** Win all the cards
**SKILLS:** Attention, observation, hand-eye coordination, reflexes

**MATERIALS:**

◊ One deck of cards with jokers removed

## How to Deal

The dealer deals out all the cards, one at a time, until the entire deck has been distributed. It doesn't matter if some players have more cards than others. Each player then stacks their cards into a single pile that remains face down in front of them.

## How to Play

1. Starting with the player to the left of the dealer and proceeding clockwise, each player turns over one card from their pile and immediately places it in the center of the table. Whenever a jack is revealed, players try to be the first to slap their hand down on it. The first player to slap the jack wins all the cards in the pile.

2. If a player slaps the center card when it is *not* a jack, they must give a card to the player who played the card. Players can continue to play even after they run out of cards; they are simply skipped when it's their turn to play a card. Play continues until one player has collected all the cards by being the last person to slap a jack when all the other players are out of cards.

# SNAP

**TWO OR MORE PLAYERS**    **FUN FOR AGES: 4+**  |  **LENGTH OF PLAY:** 10 minutes

In this quick, uncomplicated game, players race to be the first to spot matches and collect all the cards. No special skills required—just a keen eye and quick hands.

**OBJECTIVE:** Win all the cards  |  **SKILLS:** Attention, focus

**MATERIALS:**

◊ One deck of cards with jokers removed

## How to Deal

The dealer deals out all the cards, one at a time, until the entire deck has been distributed. It doesn't matter if some players have more cards than others. Each player then stacks their cards in a single pile that remains face down in front of them to form a stock.

## How to Play

1. Starting with the player to the left of the dealer and proceeding clockwise, each player turns over one card from their pile and places it face up next to the pile to form their Snap pile. When someone reveals a card that matches the top face-up card in another player's pile, the first person with one of the matched cards who says, "Snap!" wins both Snap piles and adds the cards to the bottom of their stock.

2. If a player mistakenly calls, "Snap!" when the cards do not match, that player must give the top card from their Snap pile to the player on their right.

**CONTINUED**

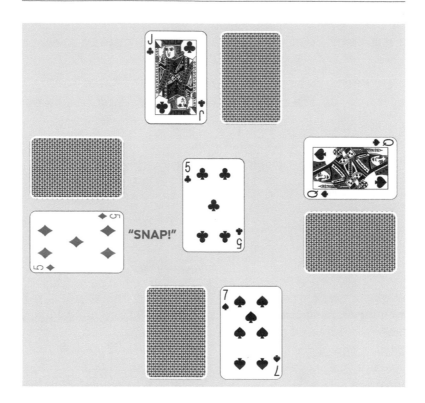

3. If two players say, "Snap!" at the same time, both piles are combined and placed in the middle with the top card face up, as shown in the picture. When a player turns over a card that matches this card, any player can call, "Snap!" and lay their hand down on top of the center pile. The first person to do so wins all the cards from the center, plus the Snap pile from the player who turned over the matching card. In the event of another tie, the new Snap pile is added to the center pile and play continues.

4. Play proceeds with the person to the left of the player who turned over the last card. If a player runs out of stock cards, they turn over the cards in their Snap pile to create a new stock. Play continues until one player has won all the cards.

# SNIP SNAP SNOREM

**THREE OR MORE PLAYERS**   **FUN FOR AGES: 4+**   |   **LENGTH OF PLAY:** 10 minutes

Snip Snap Snorem is a straightforward game with very few rules and silly proclamations that make it fun for younger kids.

**OBJECTIVE:** Get rid of all your cards

**MATERIALS:**

◊ One deck of cards with jokers removed

## How to Deal

The dealer deals out all the cards, one at a time, until the entire deck has been distributed. It doesn't matter if some players have more cards than others. Once all the cards have been distributed, players can then pick up their cards and look at them.

## How to Play

1. The player to the left of the dealer begins by playing a card face up in the center of the table. Proceeding clockwise, the next player looks to see if they have a card of the same rank. If yes, the player says, "Snip!" and plays that card on top of the first card. If the next player cannot match the rank, play passes to the next player. When the third matching card is played, the player who plays it says, "Snap!" When the fourth and final card is played, the player who plays it says, "Snorem," and they start a new round by playing any card of their choice.

2. If a player has more than one card that matches the rank of the card in play, they can play the cards all in one turn, proclaiming, "Snip," "Snap," or "Snorem" as appropriate. The first player to get rid of all their cards is the winner.

# SPEED

**TWO OR MORE PLAYERS**     **FUN FOR AGES: 4+**  |  **LENGTH OF PLAY:** 10 minutes

As its name implies, Speed is a fast game that can get pretty wild with multiple players as everyone races to get rid of their cards.

**OBJECTIVE:** Get rid of all your cards

**MATERIALS:**

◊ One deck of cards with jokers removed for every two players

## How to Deal

The dealer deals 20 cards face down to each player. Each player forms their cards into a single face-down pile, then draws the first five cards from their pile. The dealer also deals face-down reserve piles of five cards each, then places a single face-down card next to each reserve pile toward the center of the table. The face-down cards form the playing field. The number of reserve piles and single cards on the playing field should each equal the number of players. So in the example in the picture (see page 23), there are four players playing with two decks of cards.

## How to Play

1. To begin, the single cards in the playing field are flipped face up. Players play simultaneously, trying to play cards from their hands onto these foundation cards. To play a card onto the foundations, the card must be either one higher or one lower in rank than the card it is played on. Suit doesn't matter, and aces are lower than 2s. For example, on a 10 you can play either a jack or a 9, and on a 6 you can play either a 7 or a 5. As players play cards from their hands, they draw new ones from their stock to maintain five cards in their playing hand.

2. If no one can play, each player turns over a new card from the reserve piles onto the foundation piles. Game play continues until one player has played all 20 of their original cards, exhausting both their hand and their stock.

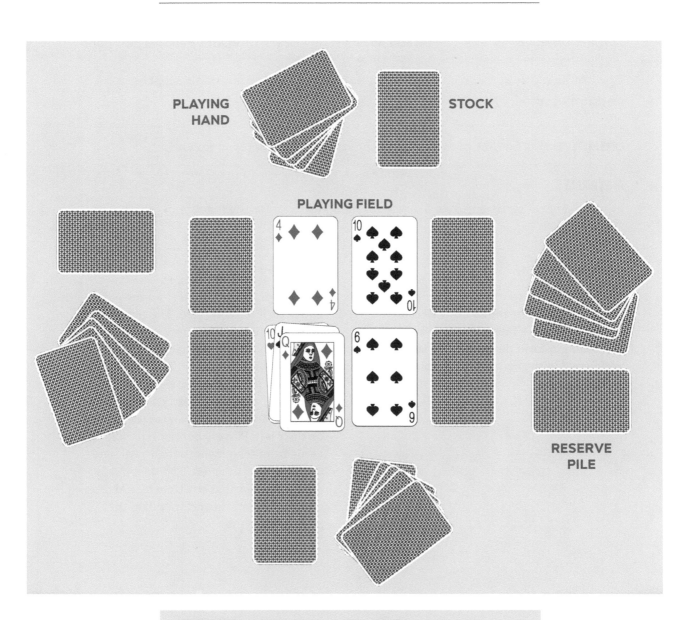

PLAYING HAND

STOCK

PLAYING FIELD

RESERVE PILE

**VARIATION:** To make the game more challenging, play with four-card hands instead of five-card hands.

# SPOONS

**THREE OR MORE PLAYERS**   **FUN FOR AGES: 4+**   |   **LENGTH OF PLAY:** 5 minutes per round

Spoons is a popular party game for people of all ages. It's basically the card version of musical chairs.

**OBJECTIVE:** Be the last player still in the game   |   **SKILL:** Observation

**MATERIALS:**

◊ One deck of cards with jokers removed, enough spoons for the number of players minus one

## How to Deal

The dealer deals four cards face down to each player. The remaining cards are placed in a single face-down pile beside the dealer to form the stock. The spoons are placed in the center of the table.

## How to Play

1. The dealer draws a card from the stock and adds it to their hand. The aim of the game play is to collect four of a kind. The dealer chooses a card to discard and sets it face down to their left. The player to the dealer's left picks up the card, adds it to their hand, and selects a card to discard, placing it face down for the player on their left. Players continue picking up cards from the player to their right and discarding to their left. The dealer can draw a new card at any time to add more cards to the round and speed up the pace of the game.

2. When one player manages to collect four of a kind, they grab a spoon from the middle of the table. All other players then immediately race to pick up a spoon. The player who fails to get a spoon is out of the game. All other players turn in their cards and spoons. One spoon is removed, and the deal passes to the left. The game continues until only one player remains. The last player is the winner.

**VARIATION:** Take the game outside and set the spoons far away from the circle. This way, players get some fresh air and exercise, too!

# STEAL THE PILE

**TWO OR MORE PLAYERS**    **FUN FOR AGES: 4+**  |  **LENGTH OF PLAY:** 20 minutes

Also known as Stealing Bundles, Steal the Pile is a fun game in which kids can pretend to be a little mischievous as they work to collect the biggest pile or bundle.

**OBJECTIVE:** Collect the most cards

**MATERIALS:**

◊ One deck of cards with jokers removed (two decks for six or more players)

## How to Deal

The dealer deals four cards face down, one at a time, to each player. Then the dealer deals four more cards face up in the middle of the table to form the playing field. The remaining cards are set aside to be used later.

## How to Play

1. The player to the left of the dealer begins by playing a card from their hand onto the playing field. If the card matches the rank of one of the cards on the playing field, the player steals the pile and places it face up in front of themselves. Players can steal piles from the playing field and also from other players. As players steal more piles, they add them to the top of the pile in front of them. If the card played doesn't match one of the cards on the playing field, the player creates a new pile. Continuing clockwise, players continue to play cards and steal piles when they are able to.

2. When all players have played all four of their cards, the remaining cards that were set aside are handed to the player to the left of the dealer. The new dealer distributes four more cards face down to each player. Play resumes as before, starting with the player to the left of the new dealer.

3. Play continues, with the deal passing every four rounds, until all the cards have been dealt. At the end of the final round, when all players have played their last hand, the player with the smallest pile receives all of the piles still left in the center playing field. The player with the most cards (that is, the biggest pile) wins.

# SWITCH

**TWO OR MORE PLAYERS**     **FUN FOR AGES: 4+**   |   **LENGTH OF PLAY:** 15 minutes

Switch, also known as Two Four Jack, is similar to Crazy Eights but includes crazier (that is, more special) cards that change up the game play, so it's almost like UNO.

**OBJECTIVE:** Get rid of all your cards

**MATERIALS:**

◊ One deck of cards with jokers removed (two decks for five or more players)

## How to Deal

The dealer deals seven cards face down, one at a time, to each player. The remaining cards are placed face down in a single pile to form the stock. The top card is turned face up and set beside the stock to form the play pile.

## How to Play

1. The player to the left of the dealer begins by playing a card from their hand onto the play pile. The card played must match the top card in the play pile in either suit or rank or be a special card.

2. Here is a list of special cards and their functions:

   ◆ Ace: The person who plays it can declare a new suit for the play pile.

   ◆ 2: When played, the next player must either draw two cards from the stock or play a 2.

   ◆ 8: When played, the next player is skipped.

   ◆ Jack: The direction of play is reversed.

3. If at any point a player cannot play a card, they must draw from the stock until they are able to play a card. If the stock runs out of cards, the top card of the play pile is set aside, and the remaining cards are shuffled to create a new stock. Play continues until one player has played all their cards. The first player to run out of cards is the winner.

**VARIATION:** Many people like to make up their own special cards (for example, when a 4 is played, the next player must draw four cards) or special rules (for example, when a player has only one card left, they must declare "last card" before another player notices, or else they must draw seven new cards).

# AGRAM

**TWO TO FIVE PLAYERS**    **FUN FOR AGES: 12+**  |  **LENGTH OF PLAY:** 5 minutes

Agram is a great introduction to trick-taking games like Euchre and Spades. It's ideal for two or four players but can be played with up to five.

**OBJECTIVE:** Win the last trick  |  **SKILL:** Strategy

**MATERIALS:**

◊ One deck of cards with jokers, all the face cards, 2s, and the ace of spades removed

## How to Deal

The dealer deals six cards to each player, three cards at a time.

## How to Play

1. The player to the left of the dealer plays a card of their choice. The next player to the left must follow suit if possible; otherwise, they can play any card of any suit. After all players have played a card, the player who has the highest card of the original suit wins the trick, removes the cards to a discard pile, and begins the next trick by playing a card of their choice. The person who wins the sixth and final trick is the winner of the game.

2. Within each suit, aces have the highest value, followed in descending order by 10, 9, 8, 7, 6, 5, 4, 3. Because the ace of spades has been removed, the 10 is the highest spade.

**VARIATION:** The most popular variation is called Sink Sink. Instead of six cards, each player receives only five (three in the first deal, then two). This version can be played by up to seven players.

# BLACKJACK

**TWO OR MORE PLAYERS**     **FUN FOR AGES: 7+**   |   **LENGTH OF PLAY:** 2 minutes

Also known as 21, Blackjack is a popular casino game that is actually a great educational game for kids and is quick and easy to play. This version has been adapted from the casino version to eliminate the dealer's advantage.

**OBJECTIVE:** Have the highest-value hand with the fewest number of cards without going over 21

**SKILLS:** Addition, decision-making

**MATERIALS:**

◊  One deck of cards with jokers removed

## How to Deal

The dealer deals two cards to each player, one at a time. The first card is dealt face up and the second card is dealt face down.

## How to Play

1. Each player looks at their face-down card. If any player has a face card plus an ace, they have Blackjack and immediately win the round. If more than one player has Blackjack, a new hand is dealt to each of them and whoever has the highest sum wins.

2. Jacks, queens, and kings are valued at ten, aces can be valued at one or eleven (player's choice), and all other card values are equal to their face value.

CONTINUED

3. If no players have Blackjack after the initial deal, play proceeds as follows, starting with the player to the dealer's left. Depending on the sum of the face-down card and the face-up card, each player decides whether or not they would like another card. If a player does not want another card, the play moves to the next player to the left. If a player wants another card, the dealer deals it to them face up. A player can request as many additional cards as they want until they decide to stand (stick with the cards they've been dealt), they reach exactly 21 (at which point they stand), or the sum of the cards exceeds 21, which is referred to as a bust.

4. After all players have bust or decided to stand, the players all reveal their cards. The player who has exactly 21 or the sum closest to 21 without going over wins the hand (so a sum of 18 beats 22). If more than one player has the same high sum, the player who got to that sum with the fewest cards wins. For example, in the picture on page 33, the player on the right wins with a total score of 19 because the bottom player went over 21 and the other two players scored 17 each. In the event of a tie, two new cards are dealt to the tied players, and the highest sum of those two cards wins.

**DID YOU KNOW?** Blackjack is one of the oldest gambling games still in existence. It's mentioned in *Don Quixote* by Miguel de Cervantes, which was published in 1605!

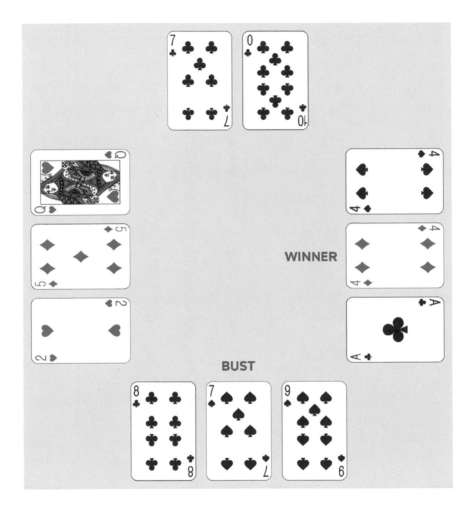

# CHINESE TEN

Chinese Ten is unlike other multiplayer card games because the goal is to capture cards from a specific tableau rather than from other players. Because players capture cards that total ten, it's also a fun way to practice basic addition with kids.

**OBJECTIVE:** Achieve the highest score by capturing cards | **SKILL:** Addition

**MATERIALS:**

◊ One deck of cards with jokers removed

## How to Deal

1. The dealer deals a total of 24 cards counterclockwise, one at a time, to each player. So in a two-player game, each player gets 12 cards; in a three-player game, each player gets eight cards; and in a four-player game, each player gets six cards. After the 24 cards have been dealt, the remaining cards are placed in a single pile, face down in the center of the table to form the stock. Then four cards are flipped over and placed in the tableau shown in the picture (see page 35).

2. In the rare event that all four cards the dealer reveals are the same rank, the dealer captures those four cards and turns over four new cards.

## How to Play

1. The player to the right of the dealer goes first. They can capture a revealed card on the table in the following ways:

   ◆ Face cards and 10s can be captured by playing a matching card (for example, a jack can capture another jack).

   ◆ Only one card can be captured at a time, with the following exception: If three matching cards are exposed (for example, three queens), a player can capture all three at once if they have the remaining matching card (the fourth queen).

   ◆ All other cards are captured by playing a card whose value added to the captured card equals 10 (so a 3 can capture a 7, since 3 + 7 = 10).

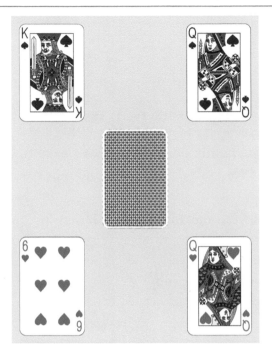

2. When capturing cards, a player takes the played card and the captured card and places them in their capture pile. Then the player replaces the captured card with a new card from the top of the stock. If the new card can capture another card, the player takes both cards and places them in their capture pile but does not replace these cards with new ones from the stock.

3. Play continues until no cards remain in the stock. Players tally their scores using these point values:

   ◆ Ace of clubs = 40

   ◆ Ace of spades = 30

   ◆ Aces of diamonds and hearts = 20

   ◆ Red 9s, 10s, jacks, queens, and kings = 10

   ◆ Red 2s through 8s = face value of the card

   ◆ Black 2s through kings = 0

4. Subsequent rounds continue until one player reaches a winning score, which is:

   ◆ Two players = 105 points

   ◆ Three players = 80 points

   ◆ Four players = 70 points

**DID YOU KNOW?** It is believed playing cards were invented by the Chinese in the ninth century during the Tang dynasty.

# CRAZY EIGHTS

**TWO OR MORE PLAYERS**     **FUN FOR AGES: 7+**   |   **LENGTH OF PLAY:** 10 minutes

Crazy Eights is a classic family card game that's easy to learn and provides plenty of opportunities for mini power trips and mock outrage.

**OBJECTIVE:** Get rid of all your cards   |   **SKILL:** Matching

**MATERIALS:**

◊ One deck of cards with jokers removed

## How to Deal

The dealer deals five cards to each player (seven cards in a two-player game), one at a time. The remaining cards are placed in a single pile face down in the center of the table to form the stock. The top card is turned over and set beside the stock to form the discard pile.

## How to Play

1. The player to the left of the dealer discards a card from their hand that matches either the rank or the suit of the top card in the discard pile. For example, if the card is a 7 of hearts, they could play any heart or any 7. If they do not have a matching card, they continue picking up cards from the stock until they draw a playable card.

2. Eights are wild and can be placed on any number or suit. For example, an 8 of spades can be played to match the 3 of hearts. The next player must then match their card to the rank or suit the 8 was meant to cover (the 3 of hearts).

3. Play continues with players matching the card at the top of the discard pile. The first player to use up all their cards wins. If the stock runs out before the game is over, the discard pile can be shuffled and used to continue play.

# DURAK

**THREE TO SIX PLAYERS**     **FUN FOR AGES: 12+**  |  **LENGTH OF PLAY:** 30 minutes

This classic Russian card game is unique in that instead of trying to win, players try to avoid losing.

**OBJECTIVE:** Avoid being the *durak* (the Russian word for "fool") by getting rid of all your cards before at least one other player
**SKILL:** Strategy

**MATERIALS:**

◊  One deck of cards with jokers removed

## How to Deal

The dealer deals seven cards to each player, one at a time. The next card is placed face up in the center of the table and establishes the trump suit for the round. The remaining cards are placed in a single pile face down crosswise on top of the trump card so it can still be seen.

## How to Play

1. The player to the left of the dealer begins by playing a card. This card is considered an attack, and now the player to the attacker's left is the defender. The defender must play a higher-ranking card of any suit or a trump card to beat the attack. If the defender is successful, the attacker can attack again with a new card that is of equal rank to at least one card already in play. For example, in a game where diamonds is the trump suit, if the attacker plays the 6 of hearts and the defender plays the 8 of clubs, the attack has been successfully defended. The attacker can attack again by playing any card that is a 6 or higher, or any trump card. For example, the attacker might play the 9 of spades. If the

**CONTINUED**

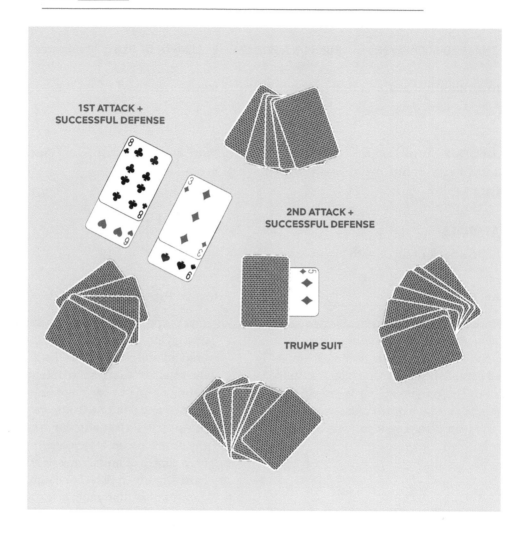

1ST ATTACK +
SUCCESSFUL DEFENSE

2ND ATTACK +
SUCCESSFUL DEFENSE

TRUMP SUIT

defender plays the 3 of diamonds, they have successfully defended against the second attack. If a defender cannot beat an attack, they pick up all the cards played during the attack and add them to their hand. The next attacker is then the player to the left of the unsuccessful defender, and their attack is directed against the player to their left.

2. The original attacker can keep attacking as long as (a) the defender continues to successfully defend against the attacks, and (b) the attacker does not play more than seven cards (or the total number of cards in the defender's hand if the defender started the round with fewer than seven cards).

3. When an attacker no longer wishes to attack, other players may attack the defender, starting with the player to the defender's left and abiding by the rules that applied to the original attacker. If at any point the defender cannot beat an attack, they must pick up all the cards that have been played and add them to their hand.

4. If a defender successfully beats all attacks, they become the next attacker and the cards that have been played are discarded. Before the next attack begins, all players must draw from the stock in turn until they each have seven cards. When the deck runs out, a new attack can begin without meeting the seven-card requirement. Play continues until only one player still has cards. This person is the durak and loses the game.

**VARIATION:** A more common version of Durak is played with a smaller deck from which the 5s, 4s, 3s, and 2s have been removed. Players each start with six cards instead of seven.

# EGYPTIAN RAT SCREW

**TWO OR MORE PLAYERS**    **FUN FOR AGES: 7+**  |  **LENGTH OF PLAY:** 20 minutes

This fast-paced game is a fun combination of luck and wits.

**OBJECTIVE:** Collect all the cards in the deck

**MATERIALS:**

◊ One deck of cards with jokers removed (two decks for more than six players)

## How to Deal

The dealer deals out the entire deck, one card at a time. Players must stack their cards in a face-down pile directly in front of themselves.

## How to Play

1. The player to the left of the dealer begins the game by flipping over the top card of their pile and putting it in the center of the table. Continuing clockwise, the next player then flips over the top card from their pile and sets it on top of the card in the middle. Play continues clockwise in a similar fashion until either a face card or an ace is played.

2. When a face card or ace appears, it is considered a challenge. The next player must try to match the card by flipping a card from their pile. If an ace was played, the next player can flip up to four cards to try to reveal another ace. If a king is played, only three cards are allowed. For a queen, the player can flip two cards. And for a jack, the player gets only one chance to match it.

3. If the challenge card is matched, it becomes a new challenge for the next player, who gets the same number of chances. The challenge continues until it reaches a player who cannot match it in the allowable number of flips. When that happens, the round ends and the last person to match the challenge card or the person who originally flipped it wins the round, takes all the cards from the center pile, and adds them face down to the bottom of their existing pile. The winner of the round begins the next round. Play continues until one player has all the cards. Some players may be out before that happens. If someone runs out of cards, they are out of the game.

**VARIATION:** Many people play Egyptian Rat Screw with slap rules. In this version, when various combinations appear in the center pile, the first player to slap the pile can claim all the cards. Combinations include doubles (for example: 7, 7), sandwich (for example: 3, 8, 3), sum of ten (for example: 4, 6), four of a kind (for example: 2, 2, 2, 2), and marriage (for example: king, queen).

# GAIN AND LOSS

**TWO OR MORE PLAYERS**    **FUN FOR AGES: 7+**  |  **LENGTH OF PLAY:** 15 minutes

This is a fun and easy way for kids to practice addition and subtraction.

**OBJECTIVE:** Get the highest score  |  **SKILLS:** Addition, subtraction

**MATERIALS:**

◊ One deck of cards with jokers and face cards removed, paper and pen for keeping score per player

## How to Deal

The cards are shuffled and placed in a single pile face down in the center of the table to create the stock.

## How to Play

1. Each player starts with 15 points and writes this number on their score sheet. The youngest player begins by drawing a card from the top of the stock. They add or subtract the value of the card from the number on their score sheet, based on the suit of the card. If the card is a black suit (that is, clubs or spades), the player adds the face value of the card to the total. If the card is a red suit (that is, hearts or diamonds), the player subtracts the face value of the card from the total.

2. Play continues clockwise, with each player drawing one card per turn, until the stock is finished. Whoever has the highest total wins.

> **VARIATION:** Play with the face cards in the deck and assign number values to them based on rank (jacks = 11, queens = 12, kings = 13).

# FAMILY GAME NIGHT TIP

### MAKE IT A PARTY

Family game nights are so much more fun when everyone gets excited about them. One of the easiest ways to accomplish this is to turn your game night into a party. It's easier than you think! You already have the key component (the entertainment); you just need party food, some music, and maybe some party favors or prizes.

Party food can be as simple as pizza and soda or breaking out some chips and dip when you sit down to play. For music, find a good playlist on Spotify or YouTube, or just turn on the family's favorite local radio station. Go for bonus points and hand out candy, gum, or something fun like glow sticks after the game as party favors. Finally, come up with a prize for the winner(s) that is easy to provide, like power over the remote control for the next week or getting to choose dinner or next week's card game.

# GO BOOM

**TWO OR MORE PLAYERS**     **FUN FOR AGES:** 7+   |   **LENGTH OF PLAY:** 5 minutes

Go Boom is the perfect easy introduction to trick-taking games, since it doesn't introduce trump cards.

**OBJECTIVE:** Get rid of all your cards

**MATERIALS:**

◊ One deck of cards with jokers removed (two decks for more than six players)

## How to Deal

The dealer deals seven cards to each player, one at a time. The remaining cards are placed in a single pile face down in the center of the table to form the stock.

## How to Play

1. The player to the left of the dealer begins by playing a card from their hand. Each remaining player plays a card that matches either the suit or the rank of the first card. So, for example, if a 9 of clubs is played, everyone must play either a 9 or a club. When every player has played a card, the trick ends. If a player cannot follow suit or rank, they must draw from the stock until they are able to play a card. If the stock is empty, the player is skipped. The player who played the highest card of the suit that was led wins the trick and gets to lead the next trick. In our example, the player who played the highest club leads the next trick. The winner of the game is the first person to play all of their cards. For added effect, the winner can throw down their cards and yell, "Boom!"

# GOLF

**TWO OR MORE PLAYERS**    **FUN FOR AGES: 7+**  |  **LENGTH OF PLAY:** 15 minutes

Golf is a popular game, though it rarely appears in card game books. Just like the sport of golf, the objective is to achieve the lowest possible score.

**OBJECTIVE:** Score the fewest points

**MATERIALS:**

◊ One deck of cards with jokers removed, paper and pen for keeping score

## How to Deal

The dealer deals four cards to each player, one at a time. The remaining cards are placed in a single pile face down in the center of the table to form the stock. The top card is turned over and set beside the stock to begin the discard pile.

## How to Play

1. Players arrange their four cards in front of themselves face down in a square (as in the picture on page 46). Each player can look once at the two cards closest to them in their square and return the cards to their original face-down position, but they may not look at the other two cards. The player to the left of the dealer begins by drawing a card either from the top of the stock or the top of the discard pile, or by knocking on the table to indicate the end of their turn.

CONTINUED

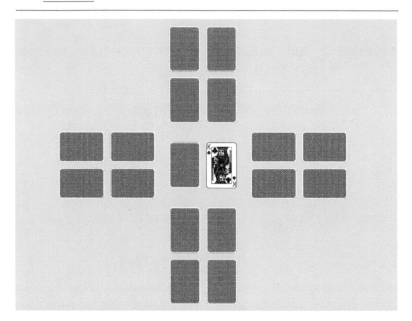

2. If a player draws a card, they look at it and then decide whether or not to replace one of the four cards in their square with the card or to discard the card. Players cannot look at any of the cards in their squares before replacing them—so they may choose to replace a card they have seen or to replace a card they have not seen. If a player does look at one of the face-down cards in their square, that card must be discarded and replaced with the card that was drawn.

3. Each player gets one turn before the round ends. At the end of the round, all players turn over the four cards in their squares and tally their scores as follows:

   ◆ Aces through 10s are worth their face value.

   ◆ Jacks and queens are worth ten points each.

   ◆ Kings are worth zero points.

4. The game consists of nine rounds. The player with the lowest total score at the end of all nine rounds wins.

# HEARTS

**THREE TO FIVE PLAYERS**     **FUN FOR AGES: 7+**   |   **LENGTH OF PLAY:** 30 minutes

Hearts is one of the best strategy card games of all time. It's the perfect balance of being fun and challenging.

**OBJECTIVE:** Achieve the lowest score   |   **SKILL:** Strategy

**MATERIALS:**

◊  One deck of cards with jokers removed, paper and pen for keeping score

## How to Deal

The dealer deals out all the cards, one at a time. In a four-player game, each player gets 13 cards. In a three-player game, the 2 of diamonds is removed, and in a five-player game, the 2s of diamonds and clubs are removed, so the cards can be distributed evenly.

## How to Play

1. The player holding the 2 of clubs (or the 3 of clubs in a five-player game) begins play. Other players must follow suit if they can. If a player does not have a card in the suit that was led, they may play any other card. The highest card of the suit that was led wins the trick, and the winner leads the next trick.

2. A player cannot lead with a heart until hearts have been "broken" in the game (that is, someone has to have played a heart during a trick when they did not have the suit that was led). Hearts cannot be broken on the first trick but can be played at any other time during the game.

CONTINUED

3. Once all the cards have been played, each player looks at the cards they won in the tricks and accrues penalty points as follows:

   ◆ Queen of spades = 13 points

   ◆ Each heart card = 1 point

4. The deal passes to the left, and the game continues until one player has accumulated 100 points. The player with the lowest score wins.

**VARIATION:** Many people include a pass round before the game begins. After the deal, each player chooses three cards from their hand to pass to an opponent (to the right on the first deal, to the left on the second deal, and across on the third deal).

# KARMA

**TWO OR MORE PLAYERS**    **FUN FOR AGES:** 7+    |    **LENGTH OF PLAY:** 30 minutes

Karma is a wonderful game that uses a custom deck of cards. I've adapted the game to a standard deck so that you can play even if you don't have a custom deck.

**OBJECTIVE:** Get rid of all your cards

**MATERIALS:**

◊ One deck of cards per every 5 players with jokers removed

## How to Deal

The player deals three face-down cards to each player. Players cannot look at these cards. Next, the dealer places one face-up card on top of each player's face-down card. Finally, the dealer deals three more cards, one at a time, to each player, which they can pick up and look at. These are the playing hands. The remaining cards are placed in a single pile face down in the center of the table to form the stock.

## How to Play

1. The player to the left of the dealer begins by playing one or more cards from their hand to start the discard pile (located beside the stock). More than one card can be played only if the cards are identical in rank (for example, a player can play two 4s at once). The player then draws from the stock until they have three cards in their hand. Play continues to the left with each subsequent player playing cards of rank equal to or higher than the top card of the discard pile. After each player has had a chance to play, the table should look similar to the picture (see page 50).

CONTINUED

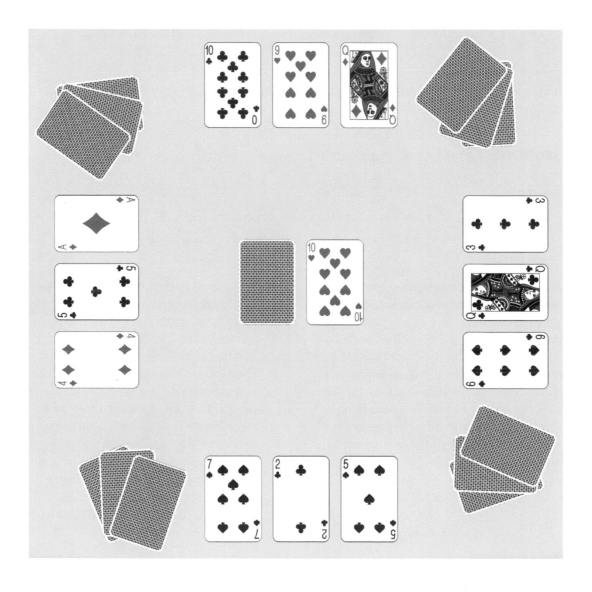

2. After drawing from the stock to form a hand of three cards, if any player is not able or willing to match or beat the previously played card, they must pick up the entire discard pile and the next player begins a new one. If at any time three cards of the same value are together in the discard pile, the person who played the third card clears the entire discard pile to the side (it is now out of play) and plays again.

3. The face-up cards in front of a player can only be played once all of the cards from their hand have been used (which does not typically happen until the stock has been exhausted). Once all of a player's face-up cards have been played, they can look at and begin playing the face-down cards. (Players cannot look at the face-down cards before playing them.) However, if they have to pick up the discard pile, they must play those cards first and use them all up before returning to the face-down cards.

4. All numbered cards in the deck retain their face value. Aces count as 1. However, face cards have the following special functions as karma cards:

   ◆ Kings let players give the entire discard pile to another player. Once played, the king is removed from play instead of being discarded.

   ◆ Queens let players play one of the table cards in front of them, even if they have cards left in their hand. If the player has any face-up table cards, one of them must be chosen; otherwise, any of the face-down cards can be selected at random.

   ◆ Jacks require the next player to play a number 5 or lower (or that next player may play a karma card instead).

5. The first person to play all their cards is the winner. Play continues to establish second and third place, and so on, until only one person remains with cards.

# KINGS IN THE CORNER

**TWO TO SIX PLAYERS**    **FUN FOR AGES:** 7+   |   **LENGTH OF PLAY:** 30 minutes

This is a great family game, since up to six people can play at once and it's easy for anyone to learn while they're playing.

**OBJECTIVE:** Score the fewest points

**MATERIALS:**

◊ One deck of cards with jokers removed, paper and pen for keeping score

## How to Deal

The dealer deals seven cards to each player, one at a time. The remaining cards are placed in a single pile face down in the center of the table to form the stock. Then, four cards are flipped over and placed at the top, bottom, left, and right of the stock to start the four foundation piles.

## How to Play

1. The player to the dealer's left starts by making as many of the following plays as they wish:

   • Playing a card from their hand onto one of the four foundation piles. The card must be one rank lower than and the opposite color of the card it is played on (for example, a red 4 can be played on a black 5). No card can be played on an ace.

   • Playing a king in one of the four corners between the foundation piles. Subsequent players can play on these corners following the same rules that apply to playing on foundation piles (as shown in the picture on page 53).

   • Moving a foundation pile to another foundation pile if the bottom card of the foundation pile being moved is one rank lower than and the opposite color of

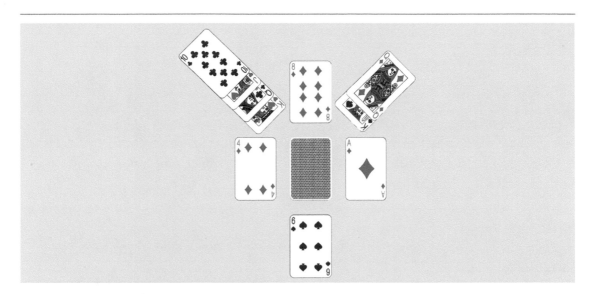

the top card of the pile where it is being moved. (For example, a pile that begins with a 10 of diamonds, followed by a 9 of clubs, 8 of hearts, and 7 of spades, can be moved to a pile that begins with a king of clubs, followed by a queen of hearts and jack of spades, because the 10 of diamonds is one rank lower than and the opposite color of the jack of spades.) Subsequent players can move entire foundation piles in a similar fashion as long as the bottom card of the moving pile is one rank lower than and the opposite color of the top card of the pile where it is being moved.

♦ Playing any card from their hand to fill a spot that has become empty due to cards being moved to another pile.

2. Once the first player has played all the cards they can or want to, they draw one card from the stock and play continues to the next player on their left. If a player cannot play any cards on a turn, they simply draw a card and end their turn.

3. Play continues until one player has played all the cards from their hand or until the stock is empty and no one is able to play. When either of these situations happen, players tally their scores. All cards still in players' hands incur penalty points. Kings are worth ten points each, and all other cards are worth one point each. The game ends when one player reaches 50 points. The player with the fewest penalty points (that is, the lowest score) wins. If no player reaches 50 points when the score is tallied, the cards should be dealt again so that play can continue following the same steps.

**VARIATION:** Instead of keeping score with pen and paper, use colored Poker chips or pennies and dimes. Each player gets the same combination and number of tokens at the start of the game and surrenders the appropriate amount at the end of each round. The game ends when someone runs out of tokens.

# NERTS

Nerts, also sometimes spelled Nertz, is a fast, fun, multiplayer version of Solitaire that is a great family game.

**OBJECTIVE:** Score the most points

**MATERIALS:**

◊ One deck of cards per player (jokers removed) with unique designs to make the decks easy to sort, paper and pen for keeping score

## How to Deal

Each player places 13 cards from their deck face down in a single pile to form their Nerts pile. Each player then flips over the top card of their pile. Beside the pile, each player deals four cards in a row face up. These cards are the foundations for each player's work piles. The remaining cards are placed next to the player face down in a single pile to form each player's stock.

## How to Play

1. Each player plays simultaneously, working to move cards from their Nerts pile onto a work pile or into the common area in the middle of the table, drawing cards three at a time from the stock to reveal new cards to put in play. To be played on a work pile, the card (either the top card from the Nerts pile or the top card of the stock draw) must be one rank lower than and the opposite color of the card it is being placed on. For example, you can place a red 3 on a black 4, or a black queen on a red king. Whenever an ace is revealed, it is placed in the common area to start a common foundation. Anyone can play on any foundation in the common area—but to play on a common foundation, a card must be one rank higher than the card on which it is placed and of the same suit. For example, you can place a 2 of hearts on an ace of hearts, and a queen of clubs on a jack of clubs.

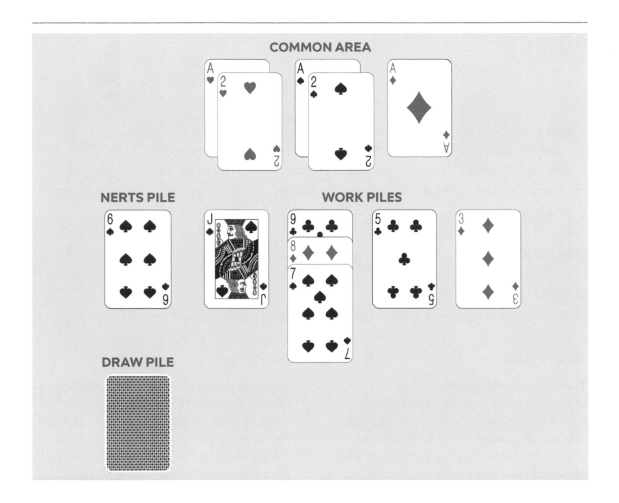

**COMMON AREA**

**NERTS PILE**

**WORK PILES**

**DRAW PILE**

**2.** Play continues until one player succeeds in removing all cards from their Nerts pile, at which point that player yells "Nerts!" to end the round. All other players must immediately stop making plays, and all players tally their scores as follows:

- The player who called "Nerts!" gets ten points.

- All other players incur one penalty point (that is, minus one point) for each card remaining in their Nerts piles.

- Each player gets one point for every card they played in the common foundations.

- The player with the highest tally wins.

# NINES

**TWO TO FIVE PLAYERS** | **FUN FOR AGES: 7+** | **LENGTH OF PLAY:** 15 minutes

Nines is a popular variation of the card game Golf. With more cards in the tableau, this version introduces some new elements that make the game even more fun.

**OBJECTIVE:** Score the fewest points

**MATERIALS:**

◊ Two decks of cards with jokers removed, paper and pen for keeping score

## How to Deal

The dealer deals nine cards, one at a time, face down to each player. The remaining cards are placed in a single pile face down in the center of the table to form the stock. The top card is turned over and set beside the stock to begin the discard pile.

## How to Play

1. Without looking at their cards, each player arranges their cards face down in front of themselves in three rows of three cards each. Then each player turns two of the cards face up. The face-up cards can be anywhere in the tableau but must be in different rows. The player to the left of the dealer begins the round by drawing a card from either the stock or the discard pile. If the player draws a card from the stock, they can either discard it or replace any card in their tableau with the card that was drawn. The card that has been replaced in the tableau is then discarded, and the card that replaced it is now face up in the tableau. If a player draws a card from the discard pile, they *must* replace a card in their tableau with that card and then discard the card that's been replaced.

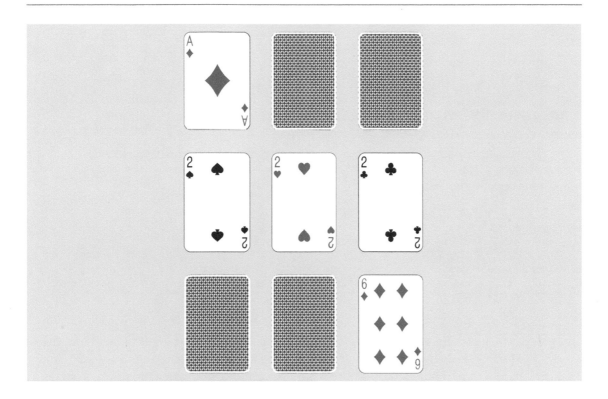

2. Players are working to get the lowest score possible by forming rows of three of a kind, which are worth zero points. (So in the example in the picture, the row of 2s is worth zero.) Players are also working to reduce their scores by including low-point-value cards in their tableau. Point values are as follows:

- Aces (worth 1) through 10s are worth their face value.

- Jacks and queens are worth ten points each.

- Kings are worth zero points.

3. The game continues until one player has turned all their cards face up. At that point, all other players turn their remaining cards face up as well so all cards are exposed. Players tally their point totals, and the player with the lowest score wins.

**VARIATION:** One fun variation is to play with jokers, which are worth minus three points each.

# 99

**THREE OR MORE PLAYERS**     **FUN FOR AGES: 7+**  |  **LENGTH OF PLAY:** 15 minutes

This is a fun and easy game that is perfect for practicing addition skills.

**OBJECTIVE:** Be the last player with a token  |  **SKILL:** Addition

**MATERIALS:**

◊ One deck of cards with jokers removed, three tokens per player (for example, pennies, buttons, or candy)

## How to Deal

Three tokens are distributed to each player. The dealer deals three cards to each player. The remaining cards are placed face down in a single pile in the middle of the table to form the stock, as shown on page 59.

## How to Play

1. Starting with the player to the left of the dealer, each player places one card from their hand into a face-up pile next to the stock. Each card added to the pile adds a value, as described in step 2. The first player announces the value of their card, then draws another card from the stock to maintain three cards in their hand. The next player adds the value of their own card and announces the new total of the pile, then draws another card, and so on. If a player cannot play a card without sending the total over 99, that player loses a token and the round ends.

2. Most cards have a value equal to their rank (for example, a 7 is worth seven points), with these exceptions:

   • 4s have no value but reverse the direction of play.

   • 9s have no value.

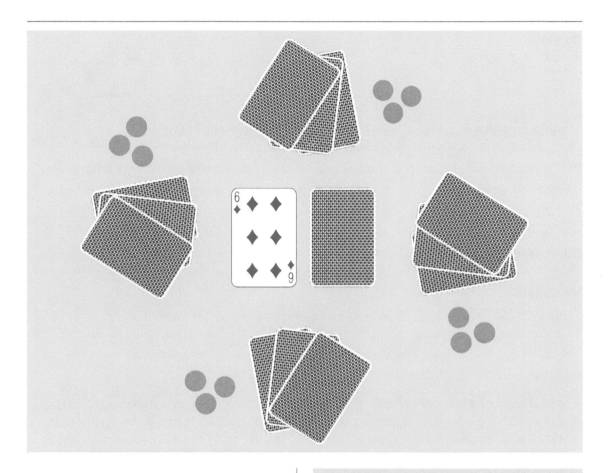

- 10s have a value of minus ten.

- Aces can be either one or eleven, decided by the person who plays it.

- Jacks and queens each have a value of ten.

- Kings have max value, meaning they immediately bring the total to 99.

3. At the end of each round, all cards are shuffled together by the next dealer (the person to the left of the last dealer). When a player has lost all three tokens, they are out of the game. Play continues until only one player has tokens. They are the winner.

**VARIATION:** Most variations of 99 eliminate or add special values and functions to cards. To make the game easier, eliminate the special functions of 4 and 9. To increase the complexity, choose a card to both add to the value and skip the next player (a common choice is 3 or 5).

# PIT

**THREE TO SEVEN PLAYERS**    **FUN FOR AGES: 7+**    |    **LENGTH OF PLAY:** 5 minutes

Pit is usually played with a specialty deck but can easily be played with a standard card deck. It's meant to imitate the chaos and excitement of the pit on a commodity trading floor.

**OBJECTIVE:** Be the first player to collect all nine cards in a suit

**MATERIALS:**

◊ One deck of cards with 10s, jacks, queens, kings, and jokers removed (two decks for more than four players)

## How to Deal

The deck is sorted into piles by suit. The dealer picks up the number of piles equal to the number of players (for example, in a three-player game, the dealer picks up three piles). The remaining piles are set aside and will not be used. The dealer shuffles together the piles they collected and deals nine cards to each player, one at a time. The dealer allows time for players to look at and sort their cards and then declares, "The pit is open."

## How to Play

1. All players play simultaneously. There are no turns. Players attempt to collect all the cards in a suit by trading with other players. Players can trade as few as one and up to four cards per trade. The number of cards being traded to another player must equal the number of cards received and must all match in suit. For example, if player A wants to trade three cards with player B, player B must have three cards to provide in exchange. If player A is trying to collect all the hearts, they may trade three diamonds from their hand to player B, hoping to gain three hearts. But players declare only the number of cards being traded, so they don't know what they are going to get in the trade. The ranks and suits are not known until the cards have been exchanged.

2. Play continues until one player "corners the market" by collecting all nine cards in one suit. They announce the commodity (that is, suit) that has been cornered and reveal their hand.

> **VARIATION:** To extend play, players can keep score. Anytime a player wins a hand, they score 100 points. The first player to score 500 points (that is, win five hands) wins the game.

# POUNCE

**TWO TO SIX PLAYERS**     **FUN FOR AGES: 7+**   |   **LENGTH OF PLAY:** 20 minutes

Like Nerts, Pounce is a multiplayer Solitaire race. Many people use the names interchangeably, but in this variation of the game, the setup is slightly different, making it just a little more challenging.

**OBJECTIVE:** Be the first player to score 100 points
**SKILLS:** Speed, hand-eye coordination

**MATERIALS:**

◊ One deck of cards per player (jokers removed) with unique designs to make the decks easy to sort, paper and pen for keeping score

## How to Deal

Each player deals out five face-down play piles in front of themselves with one card in the first pile, two cards in the second pile, three cards in the third pile, four cards in the fourth pile, and five cards in the fifth pile. When all five piles have been dealt, the top card of each pile is turned face up. Next, each player deals nine face-down cards into a single pile to form their Pounce pile and turns the top card face up. The remaining cards form each player's stock.

## How to Play

1. Players work through their stock cards by turning them over three at a time. The top card of the three must be played onto a play pile or into the common area before the card beneath it can be played. To be played on a play pile, the card must be one rank lower than and the opposite color of the card it is being placed on. So you can put a black 4 on a red 5, or a red 8 on a black 9, for example. Whenever an ace is revealed, it is placed in the common area to start a play foundation, which anyone can play on to build the pile.

2. Each player plays simultaneously, working to move cards from their Pounce pile into the foundations in the common area in the middle of the table. To play on a pile in the common area, a card must be one rank higher than the card on which it is placed and of the same suit. Cards may also be moved from the Pounce pile to an empty spot in the play pile but cannot be played onto a play pile spot that already has cards.

3. Play continues until one player succeeds in removing all cards from their Pounce pile, at which point that player yells, "Pounce!" to end the round. All other players must immediately stop making plays. All players then tally their scores as follows:

   ◆ Each player gets two penalty points (that is, minus two) for every card remaining in their Pounce pile.

   ◆ Each player gets one point for every card they played in the common area.

4. The game ends when one player accumulates 100 points. If no player reaches 100 points when the score is tallied, the cards should be dealt again so that play can continue following the same steps.

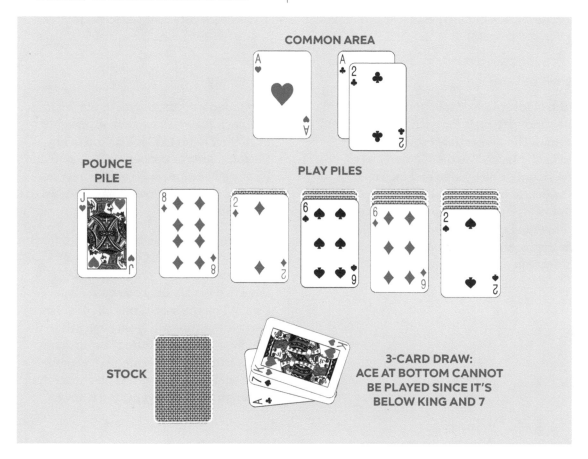

COMMON AREA

POUNCE PILE

PLAY PILES

STOCK

3-CARD DRAW:
ACE AT BOTTOM CANNOT
BE PLAYED SINCE IT'S
BELOW KING AND 7

# SOLITAIRE TWIST

**TWO OR MORE PLAYERS** | **FUN FOR AGES:** 7+ | **LENGTH OF PLAY:** 10 minutes

Solitaire Twist is a game my children made up one day when they wanted to play UNO but couldn't find the UNO deck. It's easy to learn, moves fast, and generally results in a lot of fun chatter.

**OBJECTIVE:** Get rid of all your cards

**MATERIALS:**

◊ One deck of cards with jokers removed for two to three players (two decks for four or more players)

## How to Deal

The oldest player deals first, with the deal passing to the left for each subsequent round. The dealer deals seven cards to each player. The dealer then places four cards side by side and face up in the center of the table. This is the playing field. Finally, the dealer places the remaining cards in a face-down pile next to the face-up cards to form the stock, as shown on page 65.

## How to Play

1. Beginning with the player to the dealer's left, each player must choose one card from their hand to place on top of any of the four cards in the center. The card can be any suit but must be either one rank higher or one rank lower than the card it is placed on.

2. If a player is not able to play a card from their hand, they must draw cards from the stock until they are able to play. Players can play only one card each turn. When the stock runs out of cards, remove the top card from each pile in the playing field and shuffle the remaining cards to create a new stock. The game ends when one player has no cards left in their hand. That player is the winner.

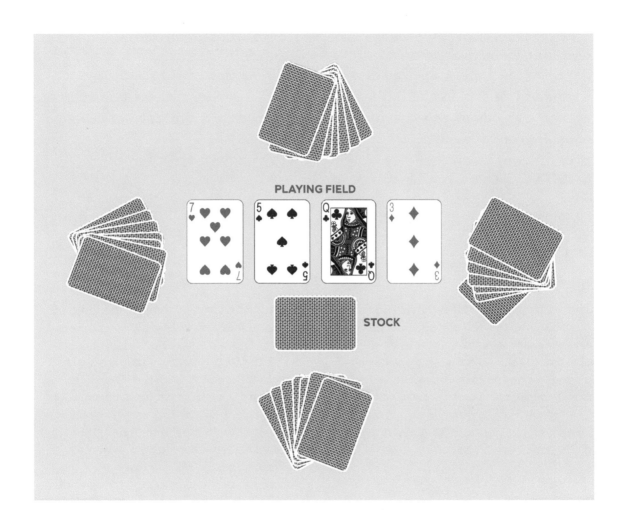

PLAYING FIELD

STOCK

**VARIATION:** To prevent players from getting discouraged if they get stuck drawing several times for a card they can play, limit the number of cards that can be drawn on any turn to five. After five, that player is skipped. To make the game easier, place six cards face up in the center instead of four. For a more challenging version, reduce the number of cards in the playing field to two.

# TOO MANY MONKEYS

**TWO TO SEVEN PLAYERS**     **FUN FOR AGES: 7+**     |     **LENGTH OF PLAY:** 20 minutes

Based on the popular specialty card game, this version has been adapted for a standard deck of cards. This is a great game for younger school-age kids who are old enough to keep track of all the special card effects but still young enough to enjoy being silly.

**OBJECTIVE:** Create a row of six face-up cards

**MATERIALS:**

◊ One deck of cards including two jokers

## How to Deal

The dealer deals six face-down cards, one at a time, to each player. Each player arranges the cards into a row in front of themselves. The remaining cards are placed in a single face-down pile in the middle of the table to form the stock. The top card of the stock is turned face up and set beside the stock to start the discard pile.

## How to Play

1. Play begins with the player who makes the best monkey noise (decided by majority vote) and continues clockwise. On each player's turn, they can either draw a card from the stock or from the discard pile. If the card is a 6 or lower (aces count as 1s), the player replaces the face-down card in the position in the row in front of them that matches the number on the card (see the picture on page 67). For example, if the player draws a 3, they count to the third card in the row (starting from their left). If the third card is face down, the player picks it up and places the 3 face up in its place. If the card they pick up is a 6 or under, the player repeats the process as long as the card that is being replaced is face down. A player's turn continues until they draw or flip over a card that cannot be placed. That card is then discarded, and the next player's turn begins.

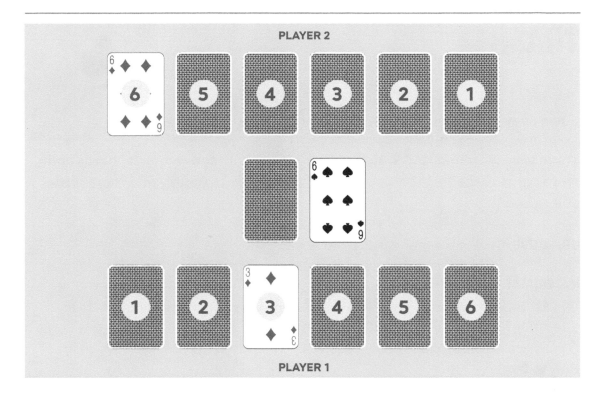

2. The first one to create a row of six cards, all face up, is the winner.

3. In addition to the aces through 6s that can be played into one of the row positions, other cards have special functions that allow them to be played during a turn.

4. Here is a list of special cards and their functions:

- 7s are Wild Monkeys and can be played as any number.

- 8s are Skip cards. When revealed, they can be placed in front of any other player so that player's next turn is skipped (after which the 8 is moved to the discard pile).

- 9s are Raccoons and allow a player to dig through the discard pile for any card they need.

- 10s can be played as any even-numbered card in a row (that is, as a 2, 4, or 6).

- Jacks can be played as any odd-numbered card in a row (that is, as a 1, 3, or 5).

- Queens and kings: when one of these is revealed, the player's turn ends immediately and the card is placed in the discard pile.

- Jokers: when a player draws or reveals a joker, they can choose one face-up card from another player's row and turn it face down.

# TRASH

**TWO OR MORE PLAYERS**    **FUN FOR AGES:** 7+    |    **LENGTH OF PLAY:** 30 minutes

Trash is very similar to Too Many Monkeys but with fewer special cards and more cards in the tableau, thus making it both easier to play and more difficult to win.

**OBJECTIVE:** Create a set of cards from ace to 10

**MATERIALS:**

◊ One deck of cards with jokers removed for two players (two decks for three or four players, three decks for five or more players)

## How to Deal

The dealer deals ten cards face down, one at a time, to each player. Each player then arranges their cards into two rows of five in front of themselves. The remaining cards are placed in a single face-down pile in the middle of the table to form the stock. The top card of the stock is turned face up and set beside the stock to start the discard pile.

## How to Play

1. The player to the left of the dealer begins by drawing a card from either the stock or the discard pile. If the card is a 10 or lower (aces count as 1s), the player replaces the face-down card in the position in the row in front of them that matches the number on the card. For example, if the player draws a 7, they count to the seventh card, starting with the top left card of the top row (so the seventh card will be the second card in the bottom row). The player picks up the card in that position and replaces it with the numbered card. Kings are wild cards and can be placed anywhere.

2. If the card they pick up is also 10 or under (or a king), the player repeats the process as long as the card that is being replaced is face down. A player's turn continues until they draw or flip over a card that cannot be placed (that is, a jack, queen, or numbered card that already has a face-up card in its position). That card is then discarded, and the next player's turn begins. The first one to place ace through 5 in the top row and 6 through 10 in the bottom row, all face up, is the winner.

> **VARIATION:** To speed up the game, deal eight cards to start instead of ten.

# VILLAGE IDIOT

**THREE TO TEN PLAYERS**　　**FUN FOR AGES: 7+**　|　**LENGTH OF PLAY:** 60 minutes

Village Idiot is a fun, extended variation of Karma. The game play is similar but with the added fun of multiple rounds and player-created rules for each round.

**OBJECTIVE:** Score the most points　|　**SKILL:** Strategy

**MATERIALS:**

◊ One deck of cards with jokers removed for three or four players (two decks for five or more players), paper and pen for keeping score

## How to Deal

The dealer deals three cards face down in a row in front of each player. Then the dealer deals one face-up card on top of each of the face-down cards in front of each player. (Each player now has six cards.) Finally, the dealer deals three cards face down to each player that will become each person's playing hand. (Each player now has nine cards.) The remaining cards are placed face down in a single pile in the middle of the table to form the stock.

## How to Play

1. Each player picks up their hand and can exchange any of the face-up cards in front of them with ones from their hand (high cards and special cards are preferred in the face-up position). The player to the dealer's left begins. If they have a 3, then they discard it immediately. If they do not have a 3, it is the next player's turn. Continue clockwise until someone is able to play a 3. If no one can play by the first player's next turn, they can play a 4. Proceed as needed, passing until someone can play, by increasing the number each round.

2. When someone is able to play the required opening card, they start the discard pile and draw a new card from the stock. Subsequent players simply need to match or beat the rank of the top card in the discard pile. For example, if the top card is a 5, a player must play a 5 or higher. If a player has multiple cards of the same rank that meet or beat the top card, they can play them all in one turn but must draw enough cards at the end of their turn so that they maintain a hand of at least three cards. For 3s through 9s, cards are ranked at their face value. Next highest are jacks, followed by queens, kings, then aces. If a player cannot (or chooses not to) play, they must pick up the entire discard pile and add it to their hand.

3. 2s are special cards. When a 2 is played, it resets the discard pile so any card can be played after it. 10s are also special cards. When played, these "burn" the discard pile, removing all cards from the round so no one has to pick them up. Four of any one rank played simultaneously or consecutively in a round also burns the discard pile.

4. Once the stock is exhausted, players continue until all but one player has succeeded in playing the remaining cards from their hand plus all the face-up and face-down cards in front of them. Players cannot play from the piles in front of them until the stock is exhausted. Also, they must play all three face-up cards before playing any of the face-down cards beneath them.

5. Keep track of the order in which people finish. The first person to finish wins the round and becomes the mayor. They score points equal to the number of players in the game. So, for example, if there are four players, the mayor scores four points. The next player to finish will sit to the left of the mayor at the start of the next round and scores one fewer point than the mayor. All other players will change their seats for the next round and earn points based on the order in which they completed the previous round—ending with the person who did not play all their cards, who will be seated to the right of the mayor and earn zero points for the round.

6. The mayor of each round gets to introduce one new rule, which will be enforced for the rest of the game. These can be as practical or silly as you want. For example, cards that have been burned can be returned to play if a 7 is played, or every time someone plays a 5, they must high-five all the other players. The game continues for a total of six rounds. The player with the highest score at the end of six rounds is the winner.

# FAMILY GAME NIGHT TIP

**MAKE YOUR OWN RULES**

Family game night should bring your family closer together. With that in mind, sit down as a family before playing and together establish some rules that will make the time more meaningful for everyone. Include silly rules along with serious ones so that they can become just as memorable as the game nights themselves.

Here are some sample rules to get you started:

- No name calling

- No cheating

- Cell phones must be left in a different room

- Winners must always take a bow

- Whenever someone says, "No fair," they must do five jumping jacks

# YAHTZEE

**TWO OR MORE PLAYERS**   **FUN FOR AGES:** 7+   |   **LENGTH OF PLAY:** 30 minutes

Most people know Yahtzee as a popular dice game. Dice are certainly just as portable as cards, but because they're also quite noisy (and easily lost), I adapted the game to be played with cards so we can play anywhere.

**OBJECTIVE:** Be the first player to score 500 points   |   **SKILL:** Decision-making

**MATERIALS:**

◊ Two decks of cards with jokers and 7s through kings removed, paper and pen for keeping score

## How to Deal

The dealer shuffles the decks together and places them face down in a single pile in the middle of the table.

## How to Play

1. The player to the left of the dealer begins by drawing five cards and lays them face up in front of themselves. They choose how many cards to keep and how many to discard, then draw cards equal to the number discarded. Again, the player chooses which cards to keep and which to discard, then draws once more (if necessary) to maintain five cards. The player then scores their hand.

2. Points are scored as follows:

   ◆ Full house (one pair + three of a kind) = 25 points

   ◆ Small straight (sequence of four) = 30 points

   ◆ Large straight (sequence of five) = 40 points

**CONTINUED**

- Yahtzee (five of a kind) = 50 points

- Random (any cards not listed above) = sum of the face value of the remaining cards, with aces = 1 point each, jacks = 11 points, queens = 12 points, kings = 13 points, and all other cards equal to their number value

3. The cards are shuffled back into the deck, and play continues clockwise in similar fashion until one player reaches 500 points.

# ANACONDA POKER

**TWO TO SEVEN PLAYERS**     **FUN FOR AGES: 12+**  |  **LENGTH OF PLAY:** 15 minutes

Also known as Pass the Trash, Anaconda Poker involves more strategic opportunities than other versions of Poker, thanks to three rounds of discards.

**OBJECTIVE:** Win the pot with the best hand or by convincing others to withdraw from the game
**SKILLS:** Observation, strategy, psychology

**MATERIALS:**

◊  One deck of cards with jokers removed, Poker chips, coins, or candy for betting

## How to Deal

The dealer deals seven cards to each player, one at a time.

## How to Play

1. After the cards are dealt, each player looks at their hand. Starting with the player to the dealer's left, a betting round begins. In a betting round, bets are placed by each player clockwise around the table. (To place a bet, you can toss coins, stars, candies, or anything else you want into a central pot.) If a player does not want to place a bet during a round and no bets have yet been placed, they "check" (that is, choose not to place a bet). After the first bet in a round, each subsequent player must either match or raise the bet. Otherwise they must fold (set their cards face down on the table and sit out the rest of the rounds in the current hand). The betting round continues until all players have bet or folded.

**CONTINUED**

2. When the first betting round has been completed, each player selects three cards to pass to the player to their left. Players look at their new cards and another betting round begins. After the second betting round, each player chooses two cards to pass to their left neighbor. Then the third betting round begins. When the third betting round ends, each player selects one card to pass to their left. The final betting round begins—ending with a showdown where each player who hasn't folded chooses their best five-card hand to reveal.

3. The player with the best hand wins the pot. Here are Poker hands in order from highest to lowest value:

   ◆ Royal flush

   ◆ Straight flush

   ◆ Four of a kind

   ◆ Full house

   ◆ Flush

   ◆ Straight

   ◆ Three of a kind

   ◆ Two pair

   ◆ Pair

   ◆ High card

> **VARIATION:** To make the game faster, reduce the number of betting rounds by allowing betting only at the beginning (before the first pass of cards) and at the end.

# BIG TWO

**TWO OR MORE PLAYERS**     **FUN FOR AGES: 12+**  |  **LENGTH OF PLAY:** 45 minutes

Big Two, also known as Deuces, is a unique blend of Poker and Crazy Eights, with an unusual ranking of the individual cards. It's a great game for anyone familiar with classic card games who is looking for a new challenge.

**OBJECTIVE:** Get rid of all your cards

**MATERIALS:**

◊ One deck of cards with jokers removed

## How to Deal

The dealer deals out the cards counter-clockwise, one at a time, to each player until all cards have been dealt.

## How to Play

1. The player holding the 3 of diamonds begins play with it. It can be played alone or as part of a combination. Play proceeds counterclockwise, with each subsequent player required to play a higher card or combination (see step 4). Any card or combination can be played as long as it beats whatever was played by the previous player. If a player cannot beat the preceding card or combination, or if the player does not want to play (to retain high cards or combinations for later), they may pass. When no further plays can be made (that is, all players pass), the trick is over and the cards are moved to a discard pile.

2. The last person who played a card begins the next trick with a new card or combination. Play continues until one player runs out of cards. CONTINUED

3. Twos are the highest-ranking cards in the game, followed by aces, then kings, queens, and so on, down to threes. The suits also have values. Spades are highest, followed by hearts, then clubs, with diamonds as the lowest. Suit rank applies only in the event of card rank ties.

4. Playable combinations include (in order of rank, starting with the lowest):

   ◆ Pairs: two cards of equal rank

   ◆ Triples: three cards of equal rank

   ◆ Straights: five cards in sequential order in several suits

   ◆ Flush: five cards in the same suit in any order

   ◆ Full house: a pair plus a triple

   ◆ Four of a kind: four cards of the same rank

   ◆ Straight flush: five cards of the same suit in sequential order

**DID YOU KNOW?** Big Two originated in China as Da Lao Er (which translates to "Big Old Two") possibly during the 1980s. It spread quickly throughout Asia and eventually made its way to Western countries. It's sometimes referred to as Chinese Poker because of the Poker combinations, even though true Chinese Poker is an entirely different game.

# CANASTA

**TWO TO SIX PLAYERS** | **FUN FOR AGES: 12+** | **LENGTH OF PLAY:** 45 minutes

Canasta is a complex strategy game that will give your brain a good workout. The rules have been simplified in this version to better suit families.

**OBJECTIVE:** Score the most points | **SKILL:** Strategy

**MATERIALS:**

◊ Two decks of cards including all four jokers

## How to Deal

The dealer deals 11 cards to each player, one at a time. The remaining cards are placed face down in the center of the table to create the stock. The top card is turned over and placed next to the stock to begin the discard pile. If the revealed card is a joker, 2, or 3, a new card must be turned over until a 4 or higher and not a joker is revealed.

## How to Play

1. The player to the left of the dealer begins play by drawing a card from the stock or by picking up the entire discard pile. To pick up the discard pile, a player must use the top card of the discard pile immediately in a meld (three or more cards of the same rank). If the player can form a meld, they must play it face up in front of themselves. (Players are not obliged to reveal melds they hold in their hand—only the ones they form from the cards in the discard pile.) The player may play as many melds as they want before discarding a single card to end their turn.

2. Anytime a player is dealt or draws a red 3, they must immediately place it face up in front of themselves and draw a new card from the stock.

CONTINUED

3. Jokers can be used to represent any card, but melds must contain at least two non-jokers. A meld of seven cards is a canasta. When a player has no cards left in their hand and has at least one canasta, the round ends. If a player runs out of cards but does not have a canasta, they must draw a card from the stock.

4. When the round ends, all players total their score from their revealed melds. (Melds still held in the hand do not count toward their score.) All players who did not go out at the end of the hand must also add up the points in their hand and deduct them from their total score.

5. First, add up the face value of all revealed cards as follows:

   • Black 3s, 4s, 5s, 6s, and 7s = 5 points each

   • Any color 8s, 9s, 10s, jacks, queens, and kings = 10 points each

   • Any color aces or 2s = 20 points each

   • Jokers = 50 points each

   • Red 3s = 100 points each

6. Using the same point system as described in step 5, deduct the face value of all cards remaining in each player's hand from their total.

7. Finally, add bonuses for any of the following:

   • Going out = 100 points (a bonus for the player who ends the round)

   • Four red 3s = 800 points

   • Each mixed canasta (with jokers) = 300 points

   • Each natural canasta (without jokers) = 500 points

8. So in the hand shown in the picture, assuming this player has gone out, they get five points for the black 5, 30 points for the three queens (10 points each), 60 points for the six 9s (10 points each), 100 points for the two jokers (50 points each), 100 points for the red 3, a 100-point bonus for going out, and a 300-point bonus for the mixed canasta. Since the player went out and did not have any remaining cards in their hand, they will not deduct anything from their score. Thus, their total score for the hand will be 695 points.

# EUCHRE

**FOUR PLAYERS**    **FUN FOR AGES: 12+**   |   **LENGTH OF PLAY:** 20 minutes

Euchre is a fun game of strategy and teamwork that can be a little confusing at first but is a breeze once you know the basics.

**OBJECTIVE:** Score ten points   |   **SKILL:** Strategy

**MATERIALS:**

◊ One deck of cards with jokers and 2s through 8s removed, paper and pen for keeping score

## How to Deal

1. The dealer deals five cards to each player, two or three at a time. The remaining cards are placed face down in a pile in the center and the top card is turned over. The dealer then asks each player, starting with the player to their left, if the player would like to declare the suit of the revealed card as trump. If a player does want the suit declared, they say, "Pick it up." The dealer picks up the revealed card into their hand and discards a different card from their hand by placing it face down at the bottom of the pile in the middle. If a player does not want the suit declared, they say, "Pass." Once trump has been chosen by any player, play immediately begins.

2. If all players pass, then another round continues with each player having the opportunity to declare any other suit trump. If no one wishes to declare trump, everyone surrenders their cards and the deal passes to the left.

3. During the game, players sitting across from each other are partners. Once a trump suit is declared, the person who chose it can opt to "go alone" if they think they can take all the tricks without their partner's help. In this case, the player's partner does not play during the round and their cards will not be played.

## How to Play

1. The player to the left of the dealer begins by playing any card. Play continues clockwise and each player must follow the suit that was led. The highest-rank card of the lead suit wins the trick. If any player does not have a card in the suit that was led, they may trump the round with any card of the trump suit or play an off-suit card. If a trump card was played, the highest-rank trump card wins the trick, as shown in the picture if diamonds is the trump suit.

2. When someone is going alone, play still progresses in clockwise order, skipping the partner of the person going alone. Thus, no matter how many people are active in a given round, there will be a total of five tricks.

3. To score the round:

   ◆ The team that declared the trump suit gets one point if they succeed in winning at least three tricks.

   ◆ The team that declared the trump suit gets two points if they win all five tricks.

   ◆ If a player who has chosen to go alone wins all five tricks, their team gets four points.

4. The deal then passes to the dealer's left, and additional rounds are played until one team scores a total of ten points and wins the game.

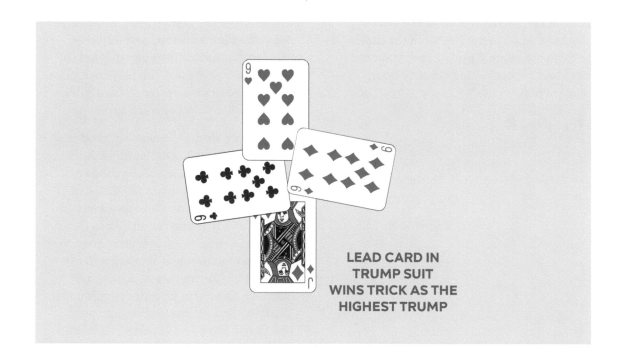

**LEAD CARD IN
TRUMP SUIT
WINS TRICK AS THE
HIGHEST TRUMP**

# MARRIAGE

**TWO TO FIVE PLAYERS**     **FUN FOR AGES: 12+**   |   **LENGTH OF PLAY:** 60 minutes

This popular Nepali Rummy variation includes a fun twist with the introduction of wild cards. I've simplified the rules to make it more family-friendly while retaining the strategic nuances of the game.

**OBJECTIVE:** Score the most points

**MATERIALS:**

◊ Three decks of cards with jokers removed, paper and pen for keeping score

## How to Deal

The dealer deals 21 cards to each player, counterclockwise and one at a time. The remaining cards are placed in a single pile face down in the center of the table to form the stock. The top card is turned over and set beside the stock to begin the discard pile.

## How to Play

1. The person to the right of the dealer begins by drawing one card from either the stock or the discard pile. They can keep the card and choose a different card to discard, or they can discard the card that was drawn. The play continues counterclockwise, with one card drawn and one discarded on each turn.

2. Players are working toward a hand of seven three-card combinations. Acceptable combinations are three cards of identical rank (for example, 4, 4, 4 of any suit) or three cards in sequence (for example, 7, 8, 9 of any suit). Aces can only be used as a 1 to start a sequence or above a king to end a sequence. Three of a kind in the same suit is called a tunnela, and if the suits differ, it is called a triplet. Sequences in the same suit are called pure and in mixed suits are called dirty.

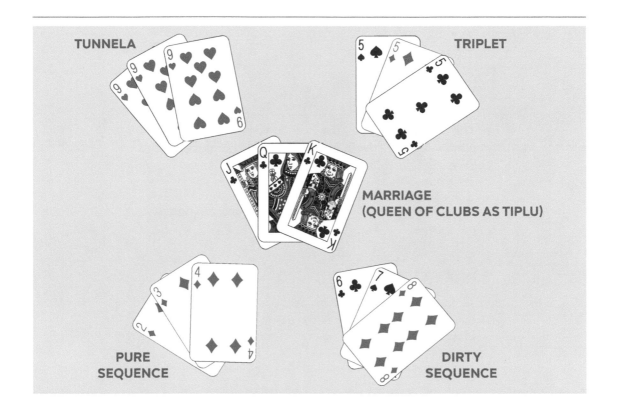

TUNNELA

TRIPLET

MARRIAGE
(QUEEN OF CLUBS AS TIPLU)

PURE
SEQUENCE

DIRTY
SEQUENCE

3. When someone has collected three tunnelas or three pure sequences (or any combination of the two), they must lay all three combinations face up on the table and select a random card from the stock. The player looks at the card without showing anyone else and places it on the bottom of the stock. That card is now the tiplu and will be the wild card for the rest of the hand. Other players can discover the tiplu only after they have played their own three combinations of tunnelas and pure sequences, after which they can look at the bottom card of the stock.

4. In addition to the combinations described, players can try to create a marriage, which is a pure sequence that contains the tiplu (that is, the wild card) and the cards of the same suit both directly above and below it in rank. (In the picture, the queen of clubs is the tiplu, so a marriage would be the jack, queen, and king of clubs.)

5. Other than the three combinations required to establish and view the tiplu, all other combinations remain in players' hands until one player is able to create four more valid three-card combinations. At that point, the player lays down all their combinations and discards their remaining card. The round ends and players tally their scores using this point system:

CONTINUED

- The player who ended the round gets ten points for each player who didn't complete the required combinations to view the tiplu and three points for each remaining player after that.

- Anyone who has a tiplu in their hand gets three points per player.

- Anyone who has a marriage in their hand gets ten points per player.

6. The game continues, with the deal passing to the right, until each person has dealt. Then the game ends and the player with the highest score wins.

# PEPPER

**TWO TO FOUR PLAYERS**     **FUN FOR AGES: 12+**   |   **LENGTH OF PLAY:** 30 minutes

Pepper is a popular game in the midwestern United States. It's easy to learn but can involve complex strategy.

**OBJECTIVE:** Be the first player or team to score 30 points   |   **SKILL:** Strategy

**MATERIALS:**

◊ One deck of cards with jokers and 2s through 8s removed, paper and pen for keeping score

## How to Deal

The dealer deals six cards, one at a time, to each player in a four-player game, or eight cards to each player in a two- or three-player game. In a two-player game, the remaining eight cards are set aside face down and remain out of play during the hand.

## How to Play

1. Starting with the player to the dealer's left, each player declares how many of the six available tricks they believe they can win with their hand. This is called a bid. A player may also choose not to bid at all and pass. If a player believes they can win six tricks, they can bid "little pepper" or "big pepper." Either pepper bid requires the bidder to win all six tricks, but in a big pepper bid, the player wins (or loses) twice as many points at the end of the round.

2. In a four-player game, the players sitting opposite each other are teammates, and their bids are combined. (For example, if one player bids one trick and the other player bids three tricks, the team's bid is four.) The player or team with the highest bid has the option to declare which suit will be trump. They can choose any suit or choose no trump.

CONTINUED

3. After everyone has bid, whoever won the bid leads the first trick with any card of their choice. Moving clockwise around the table, each must follow suit if they can. If a player cannot follow suit, they may play any card. The highest-rank trump card wins the trick. Within the trump suit, jacks are the highest rank, followed by aces, kings, queens, 10s, and 9s. If no trump cards are played, the highest card in the suit that was led wins the trick. In non-trump suits, aces are high, followed by kings, queens, jacks, 10s, and 9s.

4. When all the cards have been played, the score is tallied. If a player or team won as many as or more tricks than they originally bid, that player or team scores points equal to the number of tricks bid. So if a team bid four tricks and they won four or more, they score four points. If a player or team fails to win the number of tricks they originally bid, that player or team loses points equal to the number of tricks bid. So if a team bid four tricks and they won three or fewer, that team loses four points.

5. If a team bid little pepper and succeeds in winning all six tricks, that team scores six points. If the team bid big pepper and succeeded in winning all six tricks, they score 12 points. Likewise, if the team bids little pepper but fails to win all six tricks, the team loses six points. If they bid big pepper and fail to win all six tricks, they lose 12 points. The game ends when one player or team accumulates 30 points.

# ROOK

**FOUR PLAYERS**    **FUN FOR AGES: 12+**  |  **LENGTH OF PLAY:** 45 minutes

Rook is another game that is usually played with a specialty deck, but I've come up with this close variation that you can play with a standard deck of cards.

**OBJECTIVE:** Be the first player to score 1,000 points  |  **SKILL:** Strategy

**MATERIALS:**

◊ One deck of cards with one joker, paper and pen for keeping score

## How to Deal

The dealer deals 13 cards to each player, one at a time. The last card is placed face down in the middle of the table.

## How to Play

1. Starting with the player to the dealer's left, each player bids or passes based on how many points they believe they can win with their hand. The joker is worth 20 points, aces are worth 15 points, kings and queens are worth ten points, 5s are worth five points, and all other cards are worth zero. Bidding is trickier than adding the points one is holding, though, since players only earn points in the tricks they win. That means players must guess which cards they are holding can win tricks and whether or not they will capture cards with point values in those tricks.

2. After everyone has bid, whoever bid the most points picks up the card in the center and adds it to their hand. They then choose a card from their hand to discard by setting it aside. The winning bidder also declares the trump suit.

**CONTINUED**

3. The player to the left of the dealer leads the first trick with any card of their choice. Moving clockwise around the table, each player must follow suit if they can. If a player cannot follow suit, they may play any card. The highest-ranking trump card wins the trick. If no trump cards are played, the highest-ranking card in the lead suit wins the trick. The winner of the trick collects the cards and leads the next trick. Within each suit, ace is high, followed by king, queen, jack, 10, etc. The joker (that is, the rook) is considered a trump card but is valued as the lowest trump card.

4. When all the cards have been played, each player tallies their score based on the cards they collected in the tricks they won. The first player to score a total of 1,000 points wins.

# SPADES

**TWO OR MORE PLAYERS**     **FUN FOR AGES: 12+**   |   **LENGTH OF PLAY:** 30 minutes

This is our favorite game for teens and adults. It's the perfect combination of strategy, luck, and psychology.

**OBJECTIVE:** Be the first player or team to score 300 points   |   **SKILL:** Strategy

**MATERIALS:**

◊ One deck of cards with jokers removed, paper and pen for keeping score

## How to Deal

The dealer deals out all the cards face down, one at a time, until the entire deck has been distributed. Players can then pick up their cards and look at them.

## How to Play

1. Starting with the player to the dealer's left, each player bids based on how many tricks they believe can be won with their hand. The minimum bid is one.

2. Spades are always trump. The player to the left of the dealer leads the first trick with any non-spade card of their choice. Spades cannot be led until a trick has been trumped during the round. Moving clockwise around the table, the other players must follow suit if they can. If a player cannot follow suit, they may play any card. The highest spade (that is, trump) wins the trick. If no trump cards are played, the highest card within the lead suit wins the trick. The winner of the trick collects the cards and leads the next trick. Within each suit, ace is high, followed by king, queen, jack, 10, etc.

**CONTINUED**

3. When all the cards have been played, each player who won at least as many tricks as they bid earns ten points for each trick they bid, plus one sandbag for each trick over their bid. If a player fails to win the number of tricks they bid, that player loses ten points per trick bid. For example, if player A bids three tricks and wins four, they earn 30 points and one sandbag. Meanwhile, player B, who bid three tricks but won only two, loses 30 points. If a player accumulates ten sandbags during the game, they must deduct 100 points from their score. The game ends when one player accumulates 300 points.

> **VARIATION:** Spades is often played in teams, especially in a four-player game. Players sitting opposite each other are paired in a team, and their bids and scores are combined.

# WHIST

**FOUR PLAYERS**   |   **FUN FOR AGES: 12+**   |   **LENGTH OF PLAY:** 45 minutes

Whist is a wonderful way to introduce players to trick-taking games, since it has all the basic principles of those games without the complex bidding and rules.

**OBJECTIVE:** Be the first team to score five points   |   **SKILL:** Strategy

**MATERIALS:**

◊ One deck of cards with jokers removed, paper and pen for keeping score

## How to Deal

The dealer deals out all the cards face down, one at a time, to each player. The last card (the dealer's final card for their own hand) is dealt face up and is the trump suit for the round. After revealing it to the other players, the dealer adds the card to their hand.

## How to Play

1. The player to the dealer's left begins by playing any card to lead the first trick. Moving clockwise around the table, each player must follow suit if they can. If a player cannot follow suit, they may play any card. The highest-rank trump card wins the trick. If no trump cards are played, the highest-rank card in the suit that was led wins the trick. In all suits, aces are high and 2s are low.

2. When all the cards have been played, the score is tallied. The players sitting opposite each other are teams, so their tricks are combined. The pair that won the most tricks scores one point for each trick above six won in the round. For example, if the team won seven tricks, the team scores one point. The losing team does not score any points for the round. The first team to reach five points wins.

# Part Two

# GAMES FOR TWO PLAYERS

# BEGGAR MY NEIGHBOR

**TWO PLAYERS**  **FUN FOR AGES: 4+**  |  **LENGTH OF PLAY:** 45 minutes

Beggar My Neighbor is a great transition game to introduce young kids to basic concepts that are common in many card games. They'll learn about cards having special functions in a way that is fun and easy to grasp.

**OBJECTIVE:** Win all the cards

**MATERIALS:**

◊ One deck of cards with jokers removed

## How to Deal

The dealer deals 26 cards to each player, one at a time. Both players place their cards in a pile face down in front of them.

## How to Play

1. The player who didn't deal begins by turning the top card of their pile face up in the middle of the table. The next player then turns over the top card of their pile and places it on top of the first card. This continues until an ace or face card is played. These are court cards.

2. When a court card is played, the opponent must pay a penalty as follows:

   • Ace = four cards

   • King = three cards

   • Queen = two cards

   • Jack = one card

3. Penalties are paid by placing the required number of cards face up on the center pile. If at any point in paying the penalty the penalized player reveals a court card, they immediately stop paying the penalty and their opponent must then pay the appropriate penalty. If all the penalty cards are numbered cards, the player of the last court card gets to pick up all the cards from the center pile and add them to their pile. That player then begins play again by turning over the top card of their pile in the center of the table.

4. In the picture, player 1 has revealed a king, so player 2 has played three penalty cards. Because these penalty cards are numbered, player 1 gets to pick up all four face-up cards on the table.

5. Play continues until one player succeeds in winning all the cards.

**VARIATION:** To shorten the length of play, have players place the cards they win to the side instead of adding them to their piles. The game ends when the initial piles are depleted. The player who won the most cards wins.

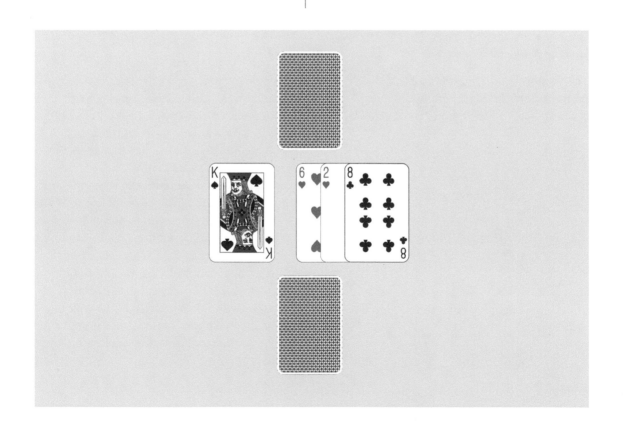

# THE BIDDING WAR

**TWO PLAYERS** | **FUN FOR AGES: 7+** | **LENGTH OF PLAY:** 15 minutes

The Bidding War is such a fun way to introduce the concept of bidding to kids. There are no Poker chips or complicated hands to memorize, just simple bids and occasional bluffing.

**OBJECTIVE:** Win the most cards | **SKILLS:** Math, psychology

**MATERIALS:**

◊ One deck of cards with jokers removed

## How to Deal

The dealer deals 26 cards to each player, one at a time. Both players place their cards in a pile face down in front of them.

## How to Play

1. The player who didn't deal begins by guessing the sum of the two top cards of both piles. (Since they haven't seen the cards, this is a totally random guess.) The dealer then makes a guess as well, but the dealer's guess must be at least two higher or lower than the non-dealer's guess. Then the players reveal the top cards from their piles and calculate the sum. Aces equal 1, jacks equal 11, queens equal 12, kings equal 13, and all other cards equal their face value. The player whose guess was closest to the sum wins the cards and sets them in a pile to the side. If the players' guesses are equally close to the sum, they engage in a bidding war.

2. In a bidding war, each player looks at the next card in their pile. The first player guesses the sum of these cards. The other player then calls or raises by guessing a higher number. If they raise, the first player then decides whether to call or raise. This continues until one player calls.

3. When the bidding war is called, the players turn over their cards and calculate the sum. If the sum of the cards is lower than the final bid, the player who made the call wins and collects all four cards. If the sum is higher than the final bid, the caller loses and their opponent collects all four cards.

4. Play continues, with players alternating who guesses the sum first, until all the cards have been won. The player with the most cards wins the game.

# GUESS MY NUMBER

**TWO PLAYERS**　　**FUN FOR AGES: 7+**　|　**LENGTH OF PLAY:** 20 minutes

This is a fun variation of the popular board game Guess Who, where players try to guess each other's numbers by asking yes-or-no questions.

**OBJECTIVE:** Collect the most cards by guessing your opponent's number correctly in the fewest number of guesses
**SKILL:** Logic

**MATERIALS:**

◊　One deck of cards with jokers and face cards removed

## How to Deal

The cards are shuffled and placed in a single pile face down between the two players.

## How to Play

1. Each player draws a card from the pile in the center. The younger player begins by asking the other player a yes-or-no question in an effort to guess what number the other player has drawn. Here are some sample questions:

   ◆　Is it an even number?

   ◆　Is it greater than __?

   ◆　Does the number have curves?

   ◆　When spelled out, does the number have an "I" in it?

2. Any question is allowed as long as it can be answered with a yes or no. Players take turns asking one question each. When a player correctly guesses the other player's number, they collect the card and the other player draws a new one. Play continues until all cards have been guessed. The player with the most cards wins.

# HIT THE TARGET

**TWO PLAYERS** | **FUN FOR AGES: 7+** | **LENGTH OF PLAY:** 15 minutes

This is a great way for kids to practice math skills. They use the cards to create math problems, which helps them view math in a creative, new way.

**OBJECTIVE:** Collect the most cards | **SKILL:** Math

**MATERIALS:**

◊ One deck of cards with jokers removed

## How to Deal

The dealer deals five cards in a row face up between the two players. The remaining cards are placed in a single pile face down near the row of face-up cards to form the stock. The top card is turned over to reveal the target as shown in the picture on page 102.

## How to Play

1. Players study the five cards in an effort to create an equation that uses two or more of them to equal the target number. The numbers can be added, subtracted, multiplied, or divided to reach the target. Numbered cards equal their face value, aces = 1, jacks = 11, queens = 12, and kings = 13. If more than two cards are used in the equation, different operations can occur between the cards and the order of operations is ignored.

2. For example, if the target number is 4, one possible equation if the exposed cards are 2, 3, 5, jack, and king is 3 + 5 ÷ 2 (3 + 5 = 8 and 8 ÷ 2 = 4). Another acceptable equation is 2 + 5 subtracted from jack (11), because 2 + 5 = 7 and 11 − 7 = 4.

CONTINUED

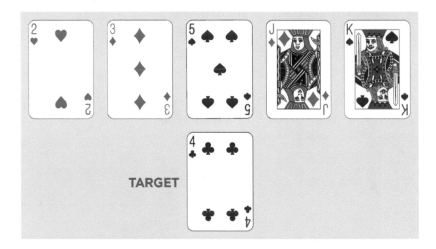

**TARGET**

3. The first person to identify a correct equation calls it out, then collects the cards used for the equation plus the target card. New cards are turned over from the stock so that there are five cards in the center and a new target card is revealed.

4. When there are no more cards in the stock, the game ends. The player who collected the most cards wins.

# OLD MAID

**TWO PLAYERS**    **FUN FOR AGES: 4+**  |  **LENGTH OF PLAY:** 15 minutes

Old Maid is a classic card game that almost everyone has played before. Usually played with a specialty deck, it's easy to play with a standard deck by adding one of the jokers as the old maid. If you don't have a joker, simply remove one of the queens from the deck, so one queen won't have a match. She is the old maid.

**OBJECTIVE:** Avoid getting stuck with the old maid at the end of the game

**MATERIALS:**

◊  One deck of cards including one joker

## How to Deal

The dealer deals out the entire deck to both players, one at a time.

## How to Play

1. Both players look at their cards and remove any matching pairs (for example, two 3s) to piles beside them face-down. If a player has three of a kind, they can make only one pair and must hold the remaining card and try to pair it later.

2. The dealer then fans out their remaining cards facing away from the other player to choose randomly from. If the other player can make a new pair with the card drawn, they match it and set it aside with their existing pairs. That player then fans out their cards facing away from the dealer so the dealer can select a random card. The dealer sets aside any pairs that are formed. Play continues until one player is left holding just the joker (the old maid). The player with the joker loses.

# SORT IT

**TWO PLAYERS**   **FUN FOR AGES: 4+**   |   **LENGTH OF PLAY:** 10 minutes

Even very young children can play Sort It, and it's amazing to see how creative they can be when coming up with their sorting rules. This is a wonderful game for parents to play with their children.

**OBJECTIVE:** Identify the opponent's sorting rule
**SKILLS:** Sorting, pattern recognition

**MATERIALS:**

◊ One deck of cards with jokers removed

## How to Deal

The dealer holds the entire deck and the other player is the guesser. At the end of the round, the players switch roles.

## How to Play

1. The dealer begins sorting cards from the deck into two piles, face up, without revealing what criteria they are using to sort. The player who didn't deal must try to figure out what the dealer's sorting rule is. The dealer must use just one sorting rule, for example:

   ◆ Red/black

   ◆ Even/odd

   ◆ Under 8/8 and over

   ◆ Four letters or fewer/more than four letters (when the number is spelled out)

2. If a player succeeds in guessing the rule, they win the round. If the player cannot figure out the sorting rule, the dealer wins.

# WAR

**TWO PLAYERS**    **FUN FOR AGES: 4+**  |  **LENGTH OF PLAY:** 15 minutes

War is a classic card game that's been around for hundreds of years, and it's the first card game most of us learn to play. Setup is easy, the rules and game play are simple, and there are plenty of ways to add your own twists for increased complexity and fun.

**OBJECTIVE:** Collect all the cards

**MATERIALS:**

◊ One deck of cards with jokers removed

## How to Deal

Deal one card to each player until all the cards in the deck have been distributed. Players should not look at their cards. Both players stack their cards in a single stock that sits face down in front of them.

## How to Play

1. On each turn, both players turn over the top card of their stock and set it in the playing field between them.

2. Whoever has turned over the higher-ranking card takes both cards and adds them to the bottom of their stock. When two cards of the same value are played, the players declare war. Each player draws three additional cards from the stock. The first two cards are played face down and the third card is played face up (see the picture on page 106).

CONTINUED

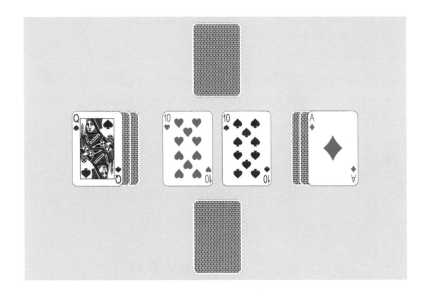

3. Between the two new face-up cards, the higher-ranking card wins (aces are higher than kings). If the cards are the same value, another war ensues, following the same process (two face-down cards, a third card revealed) to determine the winner. Wars continue until one player's revealed card is higher than the opponent's. The player of the winning card collects all of the cards from the playing field. The game ends when one player succeeds in winning all the cards.

**VARIATION:** War can easily be adapted to practice basic math skills. Instead of revealing one card each turn, players reveal two. For Addition War, the higher sum of a player's two cards wins the round. For Subtraction War, the biggest difference between the two cards wins the round. For Multiplication War, the higher product wins the round. To limit the duration of the game, it can be ended at any point agreed on by both players. The winner is the player with the most cards at that point.

# FAMILY GAME NIGHT TIP

### MAKE YOUR OWN GAMES

One of the best ways to make the most of your time together during family game night is to create a game together! You'll learn more about what types of activities each family member enjoys, plus it's a great opportunity to practice creative thinking.

The games can be as simple as a new card game (e.g., Solitaire Twist) or can involve game pieces you create. Clean out that craft supply cabinet or junk drawer, and put those items to good use! You'll be amazed at what your family can create with poster board, craft sticks, old game pieces, and plastic straws.

# DOUBLE SOLITAIRE

**TWO PLAYERS**  **FUN FOR AGES: 7+**  |  **LENGTH OF PLAY:** 10 minutes

Double Solitaire is exactly what it sounds like: Two players play to one playing field, giving each player more opportunities to play their cards.

**OBJECTIVE:** Play more cards than your opponent

**MATERIALS:**

◊ Two decks of cards (jokers removed) with designs that make them easy to distinguish

## How to Deal

1. Each player begins with one deck of cards and deals out a seven-column tableau in front of them as follows:

   ◆ Column one = one card face up

   ◆ Column two = one card face down with one card face up on top

   ◆ Column three = two cards face down with one card face up on top

   ◆ Column four = three cards face down with one card face up on top

   ◆ Column five = four cards face down with one card face up on top

   ◆ Column six = five cards face down with one card face up on top

   ◆ Column seven = six cards face down with one card face up on top

2. Each player's remaining cards form their stock.

3. The space between the two players is the playing field.

## How to Play

1. The player with the lower-rank card in their first column begins. If the cards are of equal rank, players use the top cards in the second column to determine who goes first (then the third, fourth, etc.). The first player draws three cards from their stock and places them face up in front of them into a new pile, which will form the discard pile. The top card in the three revealed cards must be played onto one of the player's columns or into the playing field before the card beneath it can be played. If the top card of the three revealed cards cannot be played, the player draws three new cards from the

stock and proceeds in similar fashion. To be played on a column, the card must be one rank lower than and the opposite color of the card it is being placed on.

2. Whenever an ace is revealed, it is placed in the playing field to start a play foundation on which either player can play. Foundation piles begin with aces and are built up in consecutive order (2, 3, etc.) in cards of the same suit. Revealed cards in columns can be moved to new columns to reveal face-down cards or open up an empty space, as long as the bottom card in the group of cards being moved is one rank lower than and the opposite color of the top card of the column to which it is being moved. For example, if a column contains a 5 of spades, 4 of hearts, and 3 of clubs, it can be moved to another column where the top card is a 6 of diamonds.

3. The first player makes all the plays and moves they can without drawing new cards from the stock. When they exhaust all possible moves, their turn ends and the other player's turn begins.

4. When a player runs out of stock cards, they gather up the cards from their discard pile (without disrupting the order) and turn the pile over to create a new stock. If a player creates an empty column by playing or moving all the cards from that column, the empty space can be filled only with a king.

5. Players continue taking turns until either one player runs out of cards or neither player can make any more moves. If one player succeeds in playing all their cards, that player is the winner. If the game ends because the players are stuck, the player who played the most cards onto foundation piles wins the game.

**VARIATION:** Instead of taking turns, players can race and play simultaneously.

# MATE

**TWO PLAYERS**     **FUN FOR AGES:** 7+   |   **LENGTH OF PLAY:** 30 minutes

Mate is a fun strategy game that gets its name from the word checkmate in chess, since the goals of the games are very similar.

**OBJECTIVE:** Score the most points   |   **SKILL:** Strategy

**MATERIALS:**

◊  One deck of cards with jokers, 2s through 6s, 8s, 9s, and jacks removed, paper and pen for keeping score

## How to Deal

The dealer deals ten cards to each player, five at a time.

## How to Play

1. The dealer begins by playing any card. The player who didn't deal must follow suit if possible. The player who played the higher-rank card (ace is high, followed by 10, king, queen, then 7) wins the trick and leads the next trick. If a player cannot match the suit that has been led, they must play a card of equal rank. In this case, the player who plays the higher suit wins the trick (clubs are high, followed by spades, hearts, then diamonds). If a player cannot match the suit or rank, they have been given mate by the other player and the round ends. Play continues until one of the players receives mate. The winner then calculates their score by multiplying the value of the card used to give mate times the number of tricks played in the round. Card values are as follows:

- ◆ Aces = 11 points

- ◆ 10s = 10 points

- ◆ Kings = 4 points

- ◆ Queens = 3 points

- ◆ 7s = 7 points

2. For example, if the dealer gives mate to their opponent on the sixth trick by playing an ace of clubs, they earn 66 points (6 × 11).

3. If a round ends without one player giving the other mate, the round is a draw and no one scores points.

4. The game continues for four rounds. The player with the higher score at the end of the four rounds is the winner.

# NIFTY 50

**TWO PLAYERS**     **FUN FOR AGES: 7+**   |   **LENGTH OF PLAY:** 15 minutes

Nifty 50 is a great way for kids to practice math skills. The game has very few rules and virtually no setup, so it's easy to learn and play.

**OBJECTIVE:** Collect the most cards   |   **SKILL:** Math

**MATERIALS:**

◊  One deck of cards with jokers removed

## How to Deal

The cards are divided evenly between both players. Each player stacks their cards in a single face-down pile in front of them.

## How to Play

1. Both players begin by drawing three cards from the top of their piles. Each player creates an equation using the three cards, trying to create a total as close to 50 as possible. The player whose total is closest to 50 wins and collects all six cards. If the totals are equal, each player keeps their own cards. Each player then draws three new cards and tries again. When all the cards have been used, the game ends. The player who has collected the most cards wins.

2. The numbers can be added, subtracted, multiplied, or divided to reach 50. Numbered cards equal their face value, aces = 1, jacks = 11, queens = 12, and kings = 13. Different operations can occur between the cards, and the order of operations is ignored.

3. For example, in the picture, the top hand can be tallied as $4 \times 11 + 1 = 45$. This would beat the bottom hand if it is tallied as $11 \times 2 + 10 = 32$.

**VARIATION:** Rather than working with each card as a standalone number, players can combine two cards to form a two-digit number (for example, a 2 and a 6 can form 26) to make more equations possible.

# SPIT

**TWO PLAYERS**  **FUN FOR AGES: 7+**  |  **LENGTH OF PLAY:** 10 minutes

Spit is a fast-paced game that often gets very lively. Players race to play their cards first, and often, cards go flying!

**OBJECTIVE:** Get rid of all your cards

**MATERIALS:**

◊ One deck of cards with jokers removed

## How to Deal

The dealer deals out 26 cards, one at a time, to each player. Each player then creates five face-down stockpiles in front of themselves. The first pile has one card, the second pile has two cards, etc. After all five piles are formed, each player flips over the top card of each pile. The remaining 11 cards are placed face down in a single pile to form each player's draw pile.

## How to Play

1. When both players are ready to begin, they say, "Spit!" and begin playing simultaneously, using only one hand each. Both players draw the top card from their draw piles and place them side by side in the common space between their stockpiles. These are the spit piles. Each player works to play all the cards from their stockpile onto the spit piles.

2. To play a card on a spit pile, it must be either one rank higher or one rank lower than the top card of the spit pile, regardless of suit. So you can play any 8 or 10 on any 9, for example. When a player plays a card from a stockpile, they may then flip over the next face-down card in the stockpile to reveal it. If one of the five stockpile spaces becomes empty, one of the face-up cards from another stockpile can be moved to that space.

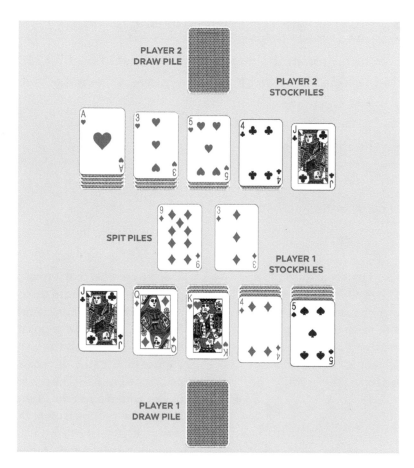

3. When neither player can make any more plays, the players say, "Spit!" again and turn over the next card from their draw piles onto the spit piles. Play continues until one of the following situations occurs:

- One player succeeds in playing all cards from their stock-piles (this player wins).

- Both players run out of draw pile cards and get stuck (the player with fewer cards left wins).

# GERMAN WHIST

**TWO PLAYERS**   |   **FUN FOR AGES: 12+**   |   **LENGTH OF PLAY:** 15 minutes

This two-player variation of the popular game Whist is perfect for pairs who love trick-taking games but don't have more players. Despite its name, the game is British, not German.

**OBJECTIVE:** Win the majority of the final 13 tricks

**MATERIALS:**

◊ One deck of cards with jokers removed

## How to Deal

The dealer deals 13 cards to each player, one at a time. The remaining cards are placed face down in a single pile between the two players to form the stock. The dealer turns over the top stock card to reveal the trump suit for the hand and sets it face up on top of the stock.

## How to Play

1. The player who didn't deal begins by playing any card from their hand. The person who dealt can then play any card from their hand but, if possible, must match the suit that was led. If that player cannot follow suit, they can play any card they choose. The trick is won by the player who played the higher trump card. If only one card is trump, that card wins the trick. If neither card is trump, the player who played the higher-rank card in the suit that was led wins the trick.

2. The trick cards are removed from the center and placed face down to the side (these tricks do not count toward the game score, so no matter who wins, they are piled together). The winner of the trick draws the top (face-up) card from the stock, then their opponent draws a (face-down) card and flips over the next card in the stock to reveal it. The face-up card on top of the stock does not change the trump. The winner of the trick leads the next trick.

3. After 13 tricks, the stock should be exhausted. Play continues as before, but the players do not draw after each trick (because there's no stock). When a player wins a trick, they collect the cards and place them to the side. These last 13 tricks will count toward the final score. When all the cards have been played, the player who won most of the final 13 tricks wins the game.

**VARIATION:** In a variation called Honeymoon Whist, the two jokers are left in the deck. The jokers should be marked in some way to tell them apart, so one can be the high joker and the other the low joker. The jokers are always trump, with the high joker being the highest-ranking trump, followed by the low joker, then the ace of the trump suit.

# GOPS

GOPS stands for Game of Pure Strategy, since players all start with the same rank cards. Players can't rely on luck to win. Instead, they need to pay close attention, keep track of which cards are left, and outwit their opponent.

**OBJECTIVE:** Score the most points in prize cards
**SKILLS:** Strategy, focus, psychology

## MATERIALS:

◊ One deck of cards with jokers and all hearts removed

## How to Deal

The diamonds are shuffled and set face down between both players to form the prize pile. Then one player gets all the clubs, and the other player gets all the spades.

## How to Play

1. One player turns over the top card of the prize pile. Each player then chooses a card from their hand to use as a bid to win the revealed prize. The player who places the highest bid (aces are high, followed by king, queen, etc.) wins the prize card, so in the picture on page 119, player 1 wins the jack. The bid cards are put down face up simultaneously. If the bids match (that is, they're a tie), the prize card is discarded. Bid cards are discarded once played.

2. Play continues until all 13 prize cards have been bid on. Players calculate the value of the prize cards they won using the following scoring system:

   ◆ Kings = 13 points

   ◆ Queens = 12 points

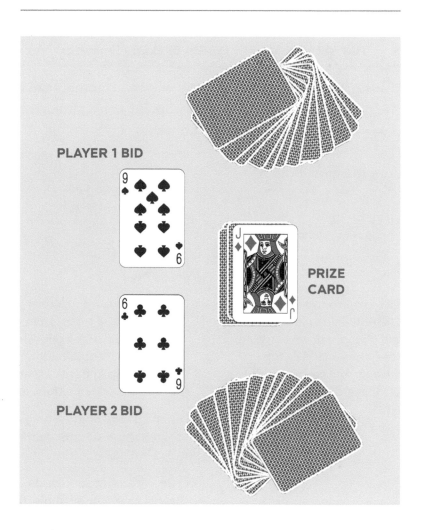

**PLAYER 1 BID**

**PRIZE CARD**

**PLAYER 2 BID**

- Jacks = 11 points

- 2s through 10s = face value

- Aces = 1 point

3. The winner is the player with the highest score.

# RUMMY

**TWO PLAYERS**    **FUN FOR AGES: 12+**    |    **LENGTH OF PLAY:** 15 minutes

Rummy is a classic, foundational card game whose principles are applied in dozens of other games. It's one of the most popular card games in the world, and once you've played it, you'll understand why.

**OBJECTIVE:** Score the most points

**MATERIALS:**

◊  One deck of cards with jokers removed

## How to Deal

The dealer deals ten cards to each player, one at a time. The remaining cards are placed in a single pile face down between the players to form the stock. The top card is turned face up and set beside the stock to form the discard pile.

## How to Play

1. The player who didn't deal goes first. They can draw a card from either the stock or the discard pile. They may then lay down any combinations from their hand face up in front of themselves. Acceptable combinations are:

   ♦ Runs: Three or more consecutive cards of the same suit (for example, 5, 6, and 7 of hearts)

   ♦ Sets: Three or four cards of the same rank (for example, three or four queens)

   Aces can be high or low (that is, queen, king, ace *or* ace, 2, 3) but cannot be used as both (so king, ace, 2 is invalid).

2. After the player lays down any combinations, they discard any card of their choice from their hand and the other

player's turn begins. If the player drew from the discard pile at the start of their turn, they cannot discard that card in the same turn it was drawn. If the player cannot lay down any combinations, they simply discard a card and play continues. If at any time the stock is depleted, the discard pile is turned face down to become the new stock.

3. Players continue taking turns drawing, playing combinations (or adding to combinations that have already been played by either player), and discarding until one player succeeds in playing all their cards, which is called going out. When a player goes out, the game ends and scores are calculated based on the cards that have been laid down by each player as follows:

◆ Face cards are worth 10 points each. 2s through 10s are face value. Aces are 1 point each

Note that cards that have been added by a player to an opponent's combination are still counted towards their own score. For this reason, these cards should be placed in front of the original player (as shown with the 9 of spades in the picture below), rather than directly on their opponent's combination. This will make scoring easier at the end of the game.

4. If a player manages to go out without previously having laid down any combinations face up on the table (that is, they have formed a hand comprised only of combinations), their points are doubled. The player with the highest score wins.

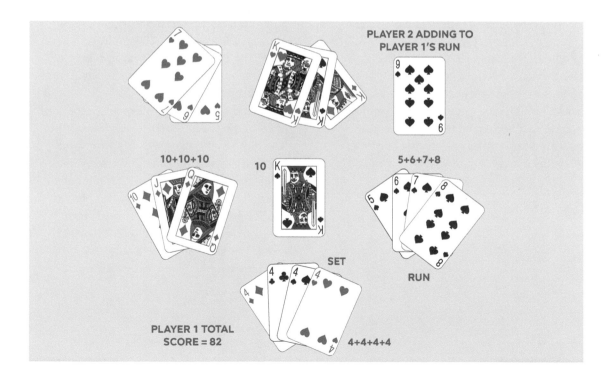

PLAYER 2 ADDING TO PLAYER 1'S RUN

10+10+10

10

5+6+7+8

SET

RUN

PLAYER 1 TOTAL SCORE = 82

4+4+4+4

# 66

**TWO PLAYERS**     **FUN FOR AGES: 12+**  |  **LENGTH OF PLAY:** 30 minutes

66, also known as Skat, is a little like the dice game Yahtzee in that you win by getting the right combination of rounds. This adds a little more luck and strategy to what would otherwise be a standard trick-taking game.

**OBJECTIVE:** Score seven game points  |  **SKILL:** Strategy

**MATERIALS:**

◊ One deck of cards with jokers and 2s through 8s removed

## How to Deal

The dealer deals six cards to each player, three at a time. The remaining cards are placed in a single face-down pile in the middle of the table to form the stock. The top card of the stock is turned face up and set beside the stock to reveal the trump suit for the round (where it will remain for the rest of the game unless swapped for a different card according to the rules outlined in step 3).

## How to Play

1. The player who didn't deal begins by playing any card from their hand. The person who dealt can then play any card from their hand. Players do not have to follow suit. The trick is won by the player who played the higher trump card. If only one card is trump, the player who played it wins the trick. If neither card is trump, the player who played the higher-rank card in the suit that was led wins the trick. The winner of the trick collects both cards and sets them face down in front of them. They draw a card from the stock, then their opponent draws a card. The winner of the trick leads the next trick.

2. When a player has both the king and queen of a suit, they can declare a marriage by revealing the two cards and then must lead with one of them. Marriages cannot be declared after the stock has been depleted.

3. After all of the cards in the stock have been drawn, players are required to follow suit if they can. At any point in the game, if a player is holding the 9 of the trump suit, they can exchange it for the trump card that was set aside before the game before leading a trick as long as they have already won at least one trick.

4. Play continues until either all cards have been played or one player who has the lead decides to close the game because they will reach 66 points or more by the end of the hand. They indicate the intention to close by turning the revealed trump card next to the stock face down on top of the stock. From that point forward, players proceed as if the stock were exhausted. They do not draw after each trick, they must follow suit if possible, and no marriages can be declared.

5. To score the round, players must first score the cards each player won in tricks, using the following point system:

   ♦ Marriage in the trump suit = 40 points

   ♦ Marriage in a non-trump suit = 20 points

   ♦ Aces = 11 points each

   ♦ 10s = 10 points each

   ♦ Kings = 4 points each

   ♦ Queens = 3 points each

   ♦ Jacks = 2 points each

6. In addition to these points, if a round ends because the stock is exhausted and not because a player closed the game, the winner of the last trick gets 10 points.

7. After each player scores their cards, the game points are awarded as follows:

   ♦ The player with the higher number of card points is the winner and gets one game point.

   ♦ If the winner has at least 66 card points and their opponent has fewer than 33 points but won at least one trick, the winner gets two game points.

   ♦ If the winner has at least 66 points and their opponent failed to win any tricks, the winner gets three game points.

   ♦ If a player closes the game but does not reach 66 points, their opponent wins and scores game points as if they won by the higher score.

8. The first player to earn seven game points wins.

# SPITE AND MALICE

**TWO PLAYERS** | **FUN FOR AGES: 12+** | **LENGTH OF PLAY:** 15 minutes

Spite and Malice is aptly named because players can, for their own future benefit, withhold in side stacks cards that help their opponent. It's all in good fun, though, so don't be surprised when this becomes a family favorite.

**OBJECTIVE:** Play all the cards from your payoff pile | **SKILL:** Strategy

**MATERIALS:**

◊ Two decks of cards with jokers removed

## How to Deal

The dealer shuffles both decks together, then deals 26 cards face down to each player, one at a time. These cards are placed in a single pile next to each player to form their payoff pile. The remaining cards are placed in a single face-down pile between the players to form the stock. The top card of each payoff pile is then turned face up and remains on the top of each pile.

## How to Play

1. The player who didn't deal begins by drawing five cards from the stock. They then play into the center as many cards as they can from their hand and the face-up card in the payoff pile. (The next card in the payoff pile is then turned face up and is playable.) To play in the center, piles must begin with an ace and then build up sequentially, regardless of suit (for example, any 3 can be placed on any 2). If no one has an ace, players draw from the stock until someone reveals an ace to start off play in the center.

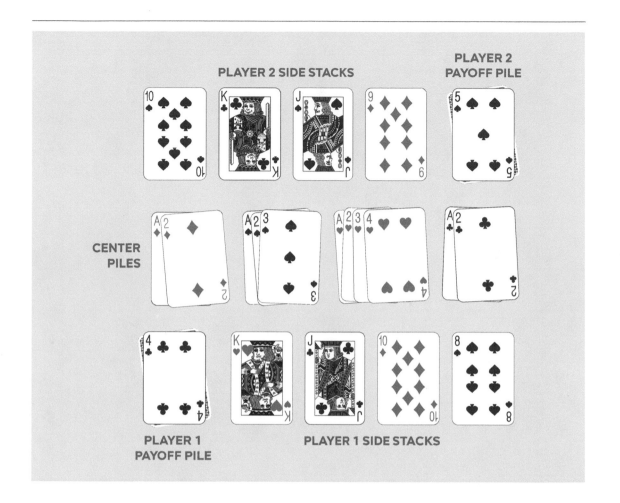

PLAYER 2 SIDE STACKS

PLAYER 2 PAYOFF PILE

CENTER PILES

PLAYER 1 PAYOFF PILE

PLAYER 1 SIDE STACKS

2. When the player can no longer make any plays to the center, they lay down one card face up next to their payoff pile to begin a side stack. A player can have up to four side stacks. There is no limit to how many cards can be added to any side stack, but only the top card in a side stack can be played (cards beneath can be played only once they are uncovered).

3. At the start of each player's turn, they must draw enough cards from the stock to provide themselves with a five-card hand. If a person plays all five cards from their hand, they draw five new cards. If the stock is exhausted, the top cards from the center piles are left in the center, but the cards beneath them are shuffled together to create a new stock. Play continues as described until one player succeeds in playing all cards from their payoff pile, at which point they win the game.

# Part Three

# GAMES FOR ONE PLAYER

# SOLITAIRE JR.

**ONE PLAYER**    **FUN FOR AGES: 4+**    |    **LENGTH OF PLAY:** 10 minutes

When little ones want to learn to play Solitaire, this easier version is a great way to introduce the concepts that are common to most single-player card games without the complexity and frustration that accompanies other versions of Solitaire.

**OBJECTIVE:** Play all cards to the four foundations

**MATERIALS:**

◊ One deck of cards with jokers removed

## How to Deal

Before shuffling, the player removes all four aces from the deck and places them in a row at the top of the playing space to form the foundation piles. Then they shuffle the deck and deal ten cards face down in a row below the aces. The player then deals another face-down card on top of each card already dealt, then one more card, face up this time, to each pile. Place the remaining cards in a single pile face down to form the stock.

## How to Play

1. Face-up cards from the columns are played to the foundation piles in sequence, building up from ace, then 2, through king. Suit does not matter. Cards can also be moved between columns if the card that is being moved is one rank lower than the card it covers when it moves. So, for example, you can move any 6 onto any 7 or any jack onto any queen. Multiple cards in a sequence can be moved at one time. If a column becomes empty, any top card in a column or sequence of cards can be moved to fill the spot. Whenever a face-down card becomes the top card in a column, it is turned face up and put in play.

2. When no more moves can be made from the cards in the columns, the player may turn over the top card of the stock. If it can't be used, it remains face up in the discard pile. The top face-up card in the discard pile can be played anytime onto a column or a foundation pile, following the rules described. Play continues until the stock is exhausted and no more moves can be made. If all four foundation piles are complete (they have kings on top, and no other cards remain in the columns, stock, or discard pile), the player wins.

**VARIATION:** As young children master this easier version of Solitaire, increase the difficulty and introduce a new skill by requiring the foundation piles to be built all in the same suit.

# CANFIELD SOLITAIRE

**ONE PLAYER**   **FUN FOR AGES:** 7+   |   **LENGTH OF PLAY:** 10 minutes

In the original version of Canfield, players would pay $50 to get the deck and then would earn $5 back for each card played to a foundation. Since the game is very difficult to beat, you can consider it a win if you play 11 cards or more!

**OBJECTIVE:** Play all cards to the four foundations

**MATERIALS:**

◊ One deck of cards with jokers removed

## How to Deal

The player deals 13 cards face down in a single pile to create the reserve. The top card is then turned face up. Next to the reserve, the player places one card face up to create the first foundation pile. The rank of that card establishes the starting rank for all four foundation piles. Finally, the player deals four cards in a row face up below the foundation pile area to form the tableau. The remaining cards form the stock, which the player holds in their hand for play.

## How to Play

1. The player works to move cards from the reserve, tableau, and stock to the foundation piles. To play on a foundation pile, a card must match the suit and be one rank higher than the top card in the foundation pile. The foundation cards are added in ascending order. For example, if the foundation is 8, the next card would be 9, then 10, jack, queen, king, ace, 2, 3, 4, 5, 6, 7—all of the same suit. New foundation piles must begin with the same rank as the initial foundation pile established during the deal. So in this example, all four foundation piles would begin with 8 and end with 7.

2. The face-up card in the reserve is in play and can be played to the foundation piles or the tableau. If a space in the tableau becomes empty, it is replaced by the top card from the reserve as well. When a card from the reserve is played, the next card in the reserve pile is turned face up.

3. Cards on the tableau can be stacked in descending order and alternating colors. So, for example, in the picture a red 4 can be placed on the 5 of spades, or a black 6 on either red 7. The player can only move the bottom card in a stack in the tableau onto a foundation pile.

4. If no cards can be played from the tableau or the reserve, the player uses the stock. To play from the stock, the player turns over three cards at a time. The top card is the only one that can be played to the tableau or to a foundation pile, according to the rules. For example, only a 6 of clubs or spades can be placed on a 7 of hearts. Cards beneath the top card of the revealed stock draw can only be played once revealed (that is, after the card above it is played).

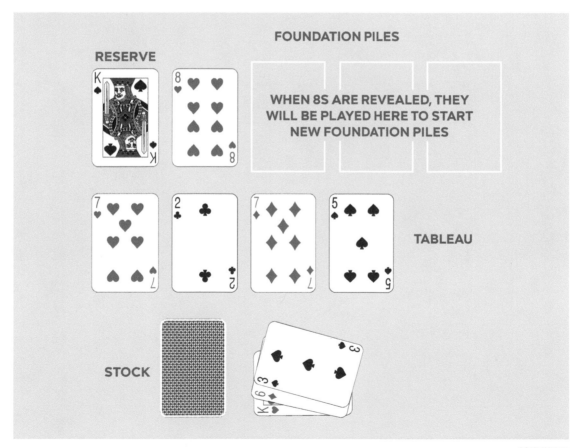

RESERVE

FOUNDATION PILES

WHEN 8S ARE REVEALED, THEY WILL BE PLAYED HERE TO START NEW FOUNDATION PILES

TABLEAU

STOCK

CONTINUED

5. If the player gets to the end of the stock, they can turn the discard pile face down to create a new stock. Play continues until the player can no longer make any moves. If they succeed in moving all cards to the foundation piles, they win.

**DID YOU KNOW?** Canfield Solitaire is named after a casino owner who claims to have invented the game but called it Klondike. Interestingly, Klondike Solitaire is another popular one-player card game but is completely different from Canfield.

# EMPEROR

**ONE PLAYER**   **FUN FOR AGES: 7+**   |   **LENGTH OF PLAY:** 20 minutes

The setup and rules for Emperor are simple, but the game is challenging to win. Players are restricted to moving one card at a time, so this game requires a good deal of luck!

**OBJECTIVE:** Play all cards to the eight foundations

**MATERIALS:**

◊ Two decks of cards with jokers removed

## How to Deal

The player deals ten piles of four cards each in a single row to form the tableau. The first three cards in each pile are dealt face down, and the top card in each pile is dealt face up. The remaining cards form the stock.

## How to Play

1. Any aces revealed can be moved to a space above the tableau to begin a foundation pile. These piles are built sequentially, by suit, from ace to 2 up to king. Face-up cards can be added to a pile if they are one rank lower than and the opposite color of the card they are played on. For example, a red 6 can be played on a black 7, or a black queen can be played on a red king. Cards within the tableau can only be moved one at a time. Whenever one is moved leaving a face-down card as the top card in the pile, the face-down card is turned face-up. Empty spaces can be filled by any card. Cards from the stock are turned over one at a time into a discard pile, from which only the top card can be played. When the stock is exhausted, it is not replenished. To continue play, the player can only work with the top card of the discard pile.

2. When no more moves can be made, the game ends. If the player has succeeded in moving all cards from the stock, discard pile, and tableau to the foundation piles, they win.

**VARIATION:** The most popular variation of Emperor is Rank and File. In this easier version, setup and game play are almost identical, but the player is allowed to move entire columns of cards within the tableau rather than being restricted to moving one card at a time.

# KLONDIKE SOLITAIRE

**ONE PLAYER**    **FUN FOR AGES: 12+**  |  **LENGTH OF PLAY:** 10 minutes

Klondike Solitaire is the most popular Solitaire game in the world and is the game most people mean when they say they are playing Solitaire.

**OBJECTIVE:** Play all cards to the four foundations

**MATERIALS:**

◊ One deck of cards with jokers removed

## How to Deal

1. The player deals out 28 cards in seven columns in the following manner:

   • Column one = one card face up

   • Column two = one card face down and one card face up on top

   • Column three = two cards face down and one card face up on top

   • Column four = three cards face down and one card face up on top

   • Column five = four cards face down and one card face up on top

   • Column six = five cards face down and one card face up on top

   • Column seven = six cards face down and one card face up on top

2. The remaining cards form the stock and are held in the player's hand.

## How to Play

1. Any ace revealed can be moved to a space above the columns to begin a foundation pile. The foundation piles are built up by suit in order from ace to 2 through king. Face-up cards in the columns can be moved to the foundation piles. They can also be moved to other columns as long as they are placed on a card that is one rank higher and the opposite color. So a red 5 can be placed on a black 6, a black 10 can be placed on a red jack, and so on. In addition, an entire column of face-up cards can be moved if the bottom card in the column is one rank lower than and the opposite color of the card to which it is moved. For example, you can move a sequence of red jack, black 10, red 9 onto a black queen.

CONTINUED

2. As face-down cards are exposed in a column, the top card is turned face up and is then in play. When no more moves can be made from the columns, the player can reveal cards from the stock by turning three cards over at a time onto a discard pile. The top card of the three is in play. The card beneath it comes into play only if it is revealed (that is, the card above it is played to either a column or foundation pile). When the stock is exhausted, the player picks up the discard pile, turns it face down, and proceeds as before.

3. Play continues until no more moves can be made. If the player can play all cards to the four foundation piles, they win.

**DID YOU KNOW?** Solitaire was originally called Patience (and still is in some parts of the world). Both terms (Solitaire and Patience) are used to describe any one-player card game or activity, including building houses out of cards.

# POKER SOLITAIRE

**ONE PLAYER**    **FUN FOR AGES: 7+**  |  **LENGTH OF PLAY:** 5 minutes

This game is for Poker fanatics who don't have any Poker buddies available.

**OBJECTIVE:** Score as many points as possible

**MATERIALS:**

◊ One deck of cards with jokers removed, paper and pen for keeping score

## How to Deal

The player shuffles the deck and places it face down in a single pile.

## How to Play

1. Drawing one card at a time, the player carefully places cards into a five-by-five grid in front of them in an attempt to create Poker hands in each row and column. The player may place a card in any open spot on the grid, but once a card has been placed, it cannot be moved to another spot.

2. When all 25 cards have been placed, the player then tallies the score as follows:

   ◆ Royal flush = 50 points

   ◆ Straight flush = 30 points

   ◆ Four of a kind = 16 points

   ◆ Straight = 12 points

   ◆ Full house = 10 points

   ◆ Three of a kind = 6 points

   ◆ Flush = 5 points

   ◆ Two pairs = 3 points

   ◆ One pair = 1 point

CONTINUED

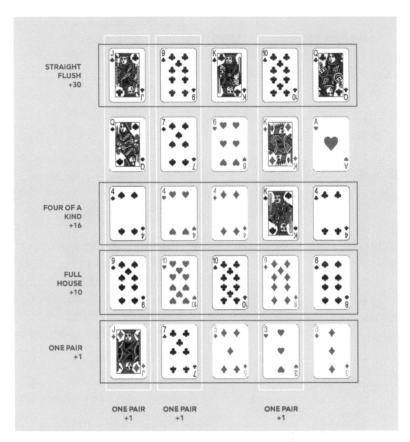

This picture shows how one would score the exposed cards. The rows marked with red boxes earn the corresponding scores shown to the left of the rows. The columns marked with white boxes earn the corresponding scores depicted at the bottom of each column.

**VARIATION:** The scoring for Poker Solitaire is based on how difficult each hand is to create in this particular game. If you're using this game to get better acquainted with Poker hands, you might prefer to score according to Poker hand rankings (in descending order): royal flush, straight flush, four of a kind, full house, flush, straight, three of a kind, two pairs, one pair.

# FAMILY GAME NIGHT TIP

### MAKE IT A TOURNAMENT

Family game nights are especially meaningful when they become a natural part of your family's routine, forming a family bond and cementing lifelong memories. To keep the weekly tradition from getting boring, add some excitement by creating a tournament.

Each week, the games can change, but the winners always earn points, which are tracked on a piece of paper or dry erase board somewhere in the house. If you don't want to track results week after week, buy or make a small trophy and hand it off each week to the new winner.

# PYRAMID

**ONE PLAYER**  **FUN FOR AGES: 7+**  |  **LENGTH OF PLAY:** 5 minutes

Pyramid is a fun Solitaire game not only because of the unique shape of the playing field but also because you can see all the cards you are targeting to remove from the beginning of the game. This creates different strategy options, depending on which variation of the game you play.

**OBJECTIVE:** Clear all cards from the pyramid  |  **SKILL:** Addition

**MATERIALS:**

◊ One deck of cards with jokers removed

## How to Deal

Deal one card face up as the apex of the pyramid. Beneath it, deal a row of two cards face up, partially covering the apex card. Continue dealing new rows in this manner, adding an additional card for each row (three cards in the third row, four cards in the fourth row, etc.) until you have created a pyramid that is seven rows tall and contains 28 cards, as shown in the picture on the next page. Set the remaining cards in a single face-down pile to the side to form the stock.

## How to Play

1. Draw one card at a time from the stock, with the aim of pairing it with an exposed card from the pyramid, which together must add up to 13. So, for example, 8 pairs with 5, 10 pairs with 3, and so on (aces = 1, jacks = 11, queens = 12, and kings = 13). Suit doesn't matter. When paired, move the cards to a waste pile. The king can be removed as a single card if exposed. Cards are exposed if no other cards are on top of them in the pyramid.

2. The top card of the waste pile is also exposed and can be paired with any exposed cards in the pyramid. Play continues until all of the cards in the pyramid have been removed (you win) or there are no more cards remaining in the stock (you lose).

**VARIATION:** To introduce more strategy and less luck into the game, stack the waste pile so that you can see each card in it rather than just the top card. All cards in the waste pile are then exposed and can be paired with each other or with exposed cards from the pyramid.

For younger children still learning to add, the game can be played to create totals of ten instead of 13. In this version, all face cards are worth ten.

Some people play Pyramid with a reserve pile. After creating the pyramid, deal six additional cards below the pyramid to keep in reserve and play anytime they are needed.

# SPIDER SOLITAIRE

**ONE PLAYER** | **FUN FOR AGES: 12+** | **LENGTH OF PLAY:** 20 minutes

Spider Solitaire is one of the easiest to adapt for different difficulty levels by simply choosing whether to treat the suits individually or by color, or to disregard them altogether. By changing this single rule at the start of each game to suit your mood, you can directly affect your chances of winning.

**OBJECTIVE:** Play all cards to the eight foundations

**MATERIALS:**

◊ Two decks of cards with jokers removed

## How to Deal

Place ten cards face down in a single row. Continue dealing face-down cards across the row of ten until each column has four cards. Deal one more face-down card to each of the first four columns, then one face-up card to each of the ten columns to complete the tableau. Place the remaining cards in a single pile face down to form the stock.

## How to Play

1. All game play takes place on the tableau. The player moves face-up cards from one column to the next in an effort to create descending sequences from kings, queens, through aces in a single color (either red or black). A card can only be moved to another card if it is one rank lower than the card it will rest on. The colors do not have to be the same suit (but if they are not, it may be harder to complete a sequence later in the game). So, you can put the queen of hearts on the king of diamonds, and the 4 of clubs on the 5 of spades. Several cards in a sequence can be moved together if they are all the same color. So you can put a black 4 and 5 together on the 6 of clubs. When a complete descending sequence is formed, it is removed from the tableau and placed in one of eight foundation piles.

2. If a column becomes empty, any top card or sequence of the same color cards can be moved to the empty space. If at any point in the game no more moves can be made, a new row of ten face-up cards is dealt from the stock and play continues as before. Play continues until the stock is empty and no further moves can be made. If all eight foundation piles have been created with complete descending sequences, the player wins.

**VARIATION:** To increase the difficulty, only allow sequences of cards in the same suit instead of simply matching the color of the suit. To decrease difficulty, disregard suits altogether so that any combination of suits can be used to create the eight sequences.

# ACCORDION SOLITAIRE

**ONE PLAYER**   |   **FUN FOR AGES: 7+**   |   **LENGTH OF PLAY:** 15 minutes

Accordion Solitaire gets its name from the way the tableau expands and contracts in a single line, similar to the movement of an accordion. It's extremely difficult to win and thus requires great patience and concentration.

**OBJECTIVE:** Get all the cards into a single pile

**MATERIALS:**

◊ One deck of cards with jokers removed

## How to Deal

Deal out the cards face up, one at a time, from left to right in a single row (or a series of rows, depending on the size of the playing space).

## How to Play

1. As the player reveals cards, any card that matches either the suit or rank of the card immediately to its left or three cards to its left can be placed on top of that card.

2. For example, in the cards in the picture on the next page, the 9 of hearts can be moved on top of the queen of hearts (matching suit immediately to the left) or the 3 of hearts (matching suit three cards to the left). If the player chooses the second option, to cover the 3 with the 9 of hearts, they could then move the queen of hearts on top of the queen of diamonds (matching rank three cards to the left). Now you'd have a pile with the 9 of hearts on top and a pile with the queen of hearts on top immediately to the left. The card on the top of the pile is

the one that counts, so you can then move the 9 of hearts pile on top of the queen of hearts pile. Close up the space to the right of the 9 and keep dealing out cards.

3. Play continues until the player can no longer make any moves. If they succeed in moving all 52 cards into a single pile, following the rules of play described, they win the game.

> **VARIATION:** To make the game more strategic, lay out all the cards in a single row (if you have a wide enough space) so you can plan all of your moves in advance.

# BELEAGUERED CASTLE

**ONE PLAYER** | **FUN FOR AGES: 12+** | **LENGTH OF PLAY:** 15 minutes

Just like a castle under siege, in Beleaguered Castle, the foundation piles are surrounded by cards all trying to make their way in. Despite the fact that all cards are revealed from the start of the game, it's a difficult game to win and requires a great deal of strategic thinking.

**OBJECTIVE:** Play all cards to the four foundations | **SKILL:** Strategic thinking

**MATERIALS:**

◊ One deck of cards with jokers removed

## How to Deal

Before shuffling, the player places all four aces in a single column in the center of the table to form the four foundations. The player then shuffles the deck and deals out six cards face up to the left and six cards face up to the right of each ace, starting closest to the ace and moving outward, overlapping the cards so that each card can be seen (as shown in the picture on the next page).

## How to Play

1. The foundation piles are built up from ace to 2 through king in the same suit. Any card that isn't covered by an overlapping card is considered revealed and can be played to a foundation pile. So in the example pictured on page 147, the 2 of diamonds can be put on the ace of diamonds. Revealed cards can also be moved to another pile and placed on top of a card one rank higher—suit doesn't matter. So, for example, the 8 of diamonds can be placed on top of the 9 of hearts, and the 7 of clubs can then be placed on top of the 8 of diamonds. The idea is to reveal cards that can be placed on the foundation piles.

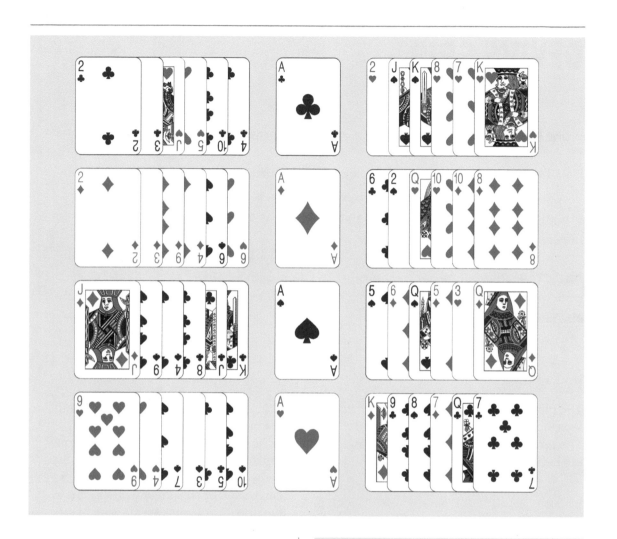

2. Only one card can be moved at a time. When a row becomes empty, any revealed card from another row may be placed there. Play continues in this fashion until the player can make no more moves. If the player succeeds in building all four foundation piles up to kings (that is, no cards remain in any of the rows), they win.

**VARIATION:** A popular (and more difficult) variation called Streets and Alleys is identical in play except the aces are not placed in advance. That means the four left rows in the tableau have seven cards each instead of six.

# DEVIL'S GRIP

**ONE PLAYER** | **FUN FOR AGES: 7+** | **LENGTH OF PLAY:** 15 minutes

Devil's Grip requires special concentration, since piles don't stack in a traditional sequence. Calling on players to think in a calculated manner and put their logic skills into action in new ways, it offers a unique game play for lovers of Solitaire games.

**OBJECTIVE:** Play all cards to the piles in the playing grid

**MATERIALS:**

◊ Two decks of cards with jokers and aces removed

## How to Deal

The player deals three rows of eight face-up cards to form the playing grid. The remaining cards form the stock and are held in the player's hand.

## How to Play

1. The goal is to play the entire deck into the piles on the grid, ending up with jacks on top in the top row, queens on top in the middle row, and kings on top in the bottom row. Any card in the grid can be swapped with any other card in the grid. Cards must be stacked in piles of matching suit, according to the specific sequences shown in the table below.

| | | | | |
|---|---|---|---|---|
| **Top row** | 2 | 5 | 8 | jack |
| **Middle row** | 3 | 6 | 9 | queen |
| **Bottom row** | 4 | 7 | 10 | king |

2. This picture shows a game in play. You can put the 5 of spades on the 2 of spades, and then the 8 of spades on top of that. You can put the king of clubs on the 10 of clubs and move them both down to the bottom row, as shown in the grid in step 1. And you can put the king of diamonds on the 10 of diamonds.

3. When an empty space is created in the grid because a card is moved onto a pile, the empty space is filled with the top card from the stock. When no more plays can be made by moving and stacking cards in the playing grid, the player begins working through the stock by turning over three cards at a time. The top card of the three can be played to the grid. Cards beneath it can only be played once revealed (that is, the card above it is played). When the stock from the player's hand is exhausted, they can pick up the pile of face-up stock cards, turn them over, and go through them again, continuing to do so as many times as possible until no more moves can be made.

4. To score, the player counts the number of cards remaining in the stock (including those in the player's hand and those that are face up on the table). Zero is a perfect score (the result of playing all cards to the grid), but many people play simply to beat their previous lowest score.

# NAPOLEON AT ST. HELENA

**ONE PLAYER** | **FUN FOR AGES: 12+** | **LENGTH OF PLAY:** 15 minutes

Napoleon at St. Helena, also known as Forty Thieves, is a very challenging game with multiple restrictions that stack the odds against you. To win, you need to focus, strategize, and hope for a good dose of luck, too.

**OBJECTIVE:** Play all cards to the eight foundations

**MATERIALS:**

◊ Two decks of cards with jokers removed

## How to Deal

The player deals ten piles of four cards each in a single column to form the tableau. All the cards are dealt face up, and in each column the cards should overlap so the player can see all the cards. The remaining cards are placed face down in a single pile to form the stock.

## How to Play

1. Any aces revealed can be moved to a space above the tableau to begin a foundation pile. Foundation piles are built sequentially, by suit, from aces up to kings. A card can be added to a pile in the tableau only if it is one rank lower than and the same suit as the card it is played on. So, for example, you can put a 7 of diamonds on an 8 of diamonds, or a 10 of spades on a jack of spades. Only the last card in a column is considered revealed and able to be played or moved. If a column becomes empty, any card can be moved to begin the column anew.

2. Cards from the stock are turned over one at a time into a discard pile, from which only the top card is considered revealed and able to be played. When the stock is exhausted, it is not replenished. To continue play, the player can only work with the top card of the discard pile.

3. When no more moves can be made, the game ends. If the player has succeeded in moving all cards from the stock, discard pile, and tableau to the eight foundation piles, they win the game.

# Index

# Acknowledgments

This book wouldn't have been possible without the wisdom and support of several important individuals. Thank you to my family for being my biggest source of inspiration and joy.

Special thanks to the friends who urged me to take this opportunity and supported me throughout the process: Raki Wright, Ashley Brownell, Carolina King, and Joyce Marrero.

I'd also like to thank my Wondermom Wannabe audience. You are the reason I am excited to get up and work each day. Your e-mails, comments, and online support make my job a joyful daily adventure.

Finally, I owe deep thanks to everyone at Callisto Media for providing me with this tremendous opportunity. Especially my editor, Adrian Potts, who patiently guided me through the process of writing a book and provided lots of encouragement and sage advice along the way.

# About the Author

Corinne Schmitt is the blogger behind Wondermom Wannabe, her platform for helping fellow moms navigate the chaotic, confusing path of motherhood with more joy and less anxiety. Raised initially in Washington, she moved to Illinois at the age of 12. After graduating high school, she continued her education at the University of Illinois, where she earned a bachelor's degree in English and a master's degree in business administration. More important, it's where she met her husband, Dan, a U.S. Marine. They've been stationed in many cities within the United States, so each of their children was born in a different state. What they've lacked in geographical stability, they've made up for in family routines and activities, with games (including family card games) playing a major role in forging a tight family bond.

CPSIA information can be obtained
at www.ICGtesting.com
Printed in the USA
JSHW062356300922
31210JS00002B/2